Knowing
Being
Doing

...and then Some

BOOKS AUTHORED OR CO-AUTHORED
BY PAUL H. DUNN

You Too Can Teach

The Ten Most Wanted Men

Meaningful Living

Win If You Will

I Challenge You, I Promise You, Vol. 1

Discovering the Quality of Success

Relationships

Anxiously Engaged

The Osmonds

The Birth That We Call Death

Goals

You and Your World

Look at Your World

Life Planning

Dimensions of Life

I Challenge You, I Promise You, Vol. 2

Horizons

Your Eternal Choice

Success Is . . .

The Human Touch

Seek the Happy Life

*Variable Clouds, Occasional Rain,
with a Promise of Sunshine*

Mothers Need No Monuments

The Light of Liberty

Christmas: Do You Hear What I Hear?

After the Storm Comes the Rainbow

No Greater Gift

Knowing
Being
Doing

...and then Some

Paul H. Dunn

BOOKCRAFT
Salt Lake City, Utah

Copyright © 1990 by Bookcraft, Inc.

All rights reserved. No part of this book may be reproduced in any form or by any means without permission in writing from the publisher, Bookcraft, Inc., 1848 West 2300 South, Salt Lake City, Utah 84119.

Bookcraft is a registered trademark of Bookcraft, Inc.

Library of Congress Catalog Card Number: 90-83210
ISBN 0-88494-773-4

First Printing, 1990

Printed in the United States of America

Contents

Preface

Some years ago as a student at the university, I was impressed with a statement made by Thomas Carlyle, the Scottish essayist and historian. Said he: "Our main business is not to see what lies dimly at a distance, but to do what lies clearly at hand." Another has said, "Today is the tomorrow we worried about yesterday." Too often in life we are tempted to concentrate on the future at the expense of the present. We live in the here and now and must daily solve and resolve the many challenges that confront us.

To me the gospel is God's plan of meeting those challenges and at the same time discovering true success and happiness. The question might well be asked, "What would you make of your life?" Many I have counseled over the years have wondered about the quality and direction of their lives, and some think they are working against great odds. It was the Apostle Paul who said, ''He which soweth sparingly shall reap also sparingly; and he which soweth bountifully shall reap also bountifully'' (2 Corinthians 9:6).

You and I, with aspiration, great determination, and understanding, can sow bountifully. A very special friend, Elder Adam S. Bennion, once said, ''Our lives are sacredly ours. They have never been lived before, and nobody else can ever live them—only we can set the bounds.''

I have long felt that religion can become too abstract if we are not careful. My own philosophy over the years, as I have met with people everywhere, has been to try to simplify gospel principles in such a way as to make them better understood and applicable. The purpose of this book is to present a number of common challenges and concerns from daily living and illustrate how gospel truths might be used to bring desired results and joy.

This work is not an official publication of the Church, but it does represent the author's thinking and ideas on solving some of life's challenges.

As on every other occasion I am again indebted to my wife, Jeanne, for her great service and editorial talents which have kept the author from returning to former literary habits developed in earlier years.

Once more I express appreciation to my daughters and their families for continued support and encouragement. And to Sharene Hansen, my able secretary over the years, I express gratitude for her care and attention to the detail and preparation of the manuscript. For my association with Bookcraft—Russell Orton, Cory Maxwell, and their staff—a relationship of friends rather than the usual publisher-author arrangements, I am grateful.

Knowing
Being
Doing

Chapter 1

Field of Dreams

Often I have the opportunity to address high school and college youth at graduations. What delightful and wonderful audiences! Each graduating class is full of excitement, emotion, and energy. One can sense and see the anticipation in the young people's expressions as they sit poised to face the future.

Commencement, as we traditionally call graduation, is the grand finale to the wonderful period spent learning and preparing. For many years leading up to this great moment, youth have had goals, purposes, objectives, and dreams. At the same time, commencement is the starting point for choice future opportunities, the possibility for the fulfillment of many dreams, and the facing of many new and meaningful challenges. I'm reminded at graduation time of a simple verse that an uncle of mine, a humorist, once penned:

> I'm well educated
> 'Tis easy to see.
> The world's at my feet,
> For I have my degree.
> M.A. will come next
> And perhaps my Ph.D.
> But I'd chuck it all
> For a good J.O.B.
>
> L. Paul Roberts

Now, that's a practical idea. And let's face it, the world does demand that we be prepared and also practical, even while we are dreaming of exciting futures. And speaking of dreams, recently one of the great movies of all time, *Field of Dreams*, played in our local theaters. It is a classic! The theme, heartwarming and tender, involves a young Iowa farmer, Ray Kinsella, who is inspired by a voice that he hears repeatedly and can't ignore and that encourages him to pursue a dream he can hardly believe could come true. Supported by his faithful wife, Annie, Ray begins the quest for this dream by turning his ordinary cornfield into a baseball diamond where the spirits of deceased professional baseball players can fulfill their hearts' desires by continuing to play ball. The climax of the story is the fulfillment of Ray's own and greatest dream, to be reunited with his professional ballplayer father (himself deceased), with whom Ray had not had—because of mistakes they both made while his father was alive—a meaningful father-son relationship.

Since first seeing the movie, I have purchased the videotape and have played it several more times.

Each time, I come away with the deep impression that, while Ray's dream involved just a cornfield, the future of our youth and what they make of themselves depends on fields of many kinds.

The Field of Knowing

Mortimer Adler said: "Man's greatness lies in his power of thought." Thorndike added: "The aim of education is, as we have seen, to change human beings for the better, so that they will have more humane and useful wants and be more able to satisfy them." David O. McKay stated further: "The aim of education is to develop resources in the child that will contribute to his well-being as long as life endures; to develop power of self-mastery that he may never be a slave to indulgence or other weaknesses, to develop virile manhood, beautiful womanhood that in every child and every youth may be found at least the promise of a friend, a companion, one who later may be fit for husband or wife, an exemplary father or a loving, intelligent mother, one who can face life with courage, meet disaster with fortitude, and face death without fear" (*Gospel Ideals* [Salt Lake City: Improvement Era, 1953], p. 436).

I learned early in my education that the next best thing to knowing a fact is wanting to know it and then knowing where to find it. A wise teacher has said: "To not know is no sin; to not ask is." And an old African proverb states: "Not to know is bad; not to wish to know is worse."

Not long ago I was visiting with the president of a major U.S. corporation about his company's hiring policies. He said to me: "If I could have only two qualities on which to judge a person's promise and abilities, I would choose *curiosity* and *determination.*

Only the curious will learn, and only the resolute overcome the obstacles to learning. Curiosity and determination—these I regard as more important than a person's grades or I.Q.''

Let's be curious and determined in all that we do. Go to school, keep learning, and develop an open mind.

The Field of Being

Many years ago a wonderful teacher instilled in me a desire to collect and memorize inspirational thoughts. That habit remains with me to this day. For instance: "Avoid suspicion. When walking through your neighbor's melon patch, don't bend over to tie your shoes." Or, "Vows made in storms are forgotten in calms." And, "A man 'convinced' against his will is of the same opinion still!" Because of this little habit of collecting "gem thoughts," I often read signs and notices as I travel to and fro. For years I have had an interest in studying the signs posted outside various churches to identify the clergy and the sermon for the coming week. Here are a few I think would be worth listening to:

1. Knowing the scriptures is one thing; knowing the author is another.
2. The Bible helps when it's open.
3. Don't expect a million-dollar answer to a ten-cent prayer.
4. To master the Bible, the Bible must first master you.
5. No man ever got lost on a straight road.
6. Feed your faith, and your doubts will starve to death.

7. You can't possibly stumble if you are on your knees.
8. It's right to be contented with what you have but not with what you are.
9. We can pray, believe, and receive, or we can pray, doubt, and do without.
10. If you stand for nothing you will fall for anything.

I think one of the best "sermons" I ever saw was on a traffic sign. It read simply: KEEP RIGHT. While signs and sermons are wonderful to read or hear and to ponder, they are of no value unless put to use. Everything that grows changes. It's what you learn after you know it all that counts. So it is with faith. What a person believes has everything to do with what a person is and becomes.

David O. McKay has said: "Faith is a divine gift given unto those who desire and work for it. Faith gives us an assurance of the unseen and is the power by which the soul is opened to truth. We walk by faith in mortality and not by sight as we did in the spirit world before earthly birth; therefore without face-to-face knowledge of God, we cling to the words given by those who bare record of Him, that He lives and guides our destinies. Children should learn faith as they grow, for they learn little in adulthood if not given that start in youth. The world's greatest need is an unwavering faith in a divine providence."

Let me conclude with this observation: In my personal library at home, I have a special shelf which holds all of the textbooks that were required as I sought three different college and university degrees. The books are scholarly and impressive and contain much information for which I was accountable to my professors. Interesting is the fact that a good deal of the material contained in those volumes is no longer valid. Many theories have been proven wrong and new scientific data has changed our views in science, math, and the human disciplines. One of my chemistry books states emphatically that an atom cannot be split. One day in August 1945, while I was serving my country in the Philippines, an atom bomb was dropped which ended a war and proved a so-called law of science wrong.

Near this shelf of great textbooks I have displayed the standard works of the Church. Isn't it interesting that the contents of these volumes are as valid as when they were first recorded?

I am not suggesting we should not read and learn from the great minds of the world, but how important it is to keep things in perspective. What a wonderful thing it would be if each of us could read the following at least once a month:

A. The Ten Commandments (Just think, there are over thirty-five million laws trying to enforce ten commandments!)
B. The Beatitudes
C. The Thirteen Articles of Faith
D. The Word of Wisdom

Knowing is gathering truths such as these and many more. Being what you want to be and what you can be depends on internalizing these truths.

My father often taught:

If you want to plant for a year—plant grain.
If you want to plant for ten years—plant a tree.
If you want to plant for eternity—plant faith and a
testimony.

The Field of Doing

It has been said: "If you figure you're going nowhere and you don't do anything about it, you'll get there." Remember: "A ship in the harbor is safe, but that is not what ships are built for." Did you know that

There are two kinds of people on earth today;
Just two kinds of people, no more, I say.

Not the sinner and saint, for it's well understood,
The good are half bad, and the bad are
      half good. . . .

No; the two kinds of people on earth I mean,
Are the people who lift, and the people who lean.

(From Ella Wheeler Wilcox, "Leaners or Lifters," in James Dalton Morrison, ed., *Masterpieces of Religious Verse* [New York: Harper and Row, 1948], pp. 421–22.)

I have noticed that for the most part young people want to be professionals in their fields. Professionals are people who can do their jobs when they don't feel like it. Amateurs are people who *can't* do their jobs when they *do* feel like it. One of the great deterrents to becoming professional, however, is the lack of proper training (education) coupled with an abundance of critics whose negative attitudes tend to discourage a person. Be careful of cynicism. It's all about. Every form of media plays on the negative and it can affect all ages. Consider the young lad in James T. Fields's "The Owl Critic":

"Who stuffed that white owl?" No one spoke in
      the shop;

The barber was busy, and he couldn't stop;
The customers, waiting their turns, were reading
The *Daily*, the *Herald*, the *Post*, little heeding
The young man who blurted out such a blunt
    question;
Not one raised a head, or even made a
    suggestion;
    And the barber kept on shaving.

"Don't you see, Mister Brown,"
Cried the youth with a frown,
"How wrong the whole thing is,
How preposterous each wing is,
How flattened the head, how jammed down the
    neck is—
In short, the whole owl, what an ignorant wreck
    'tis! . . .

"No owl in this world
Ever had his claws curled,
Ever had his legs slanted,
Ever had his bill canted,
Ever had his neck screwed
Into that attitude.
He can't do it, because
'Tis against all bird laws.
Anatomy teaches,
Ornithology preaches,
An owl has a toe
That can't turn out so!
I've made the white owl my study for years,
And to see such a job almost moves me to tears!

"Mister Brown, I'm amazed
You should be so crazed
As to put up a bird
In that posture absurd!
To look at that owl really brings on a dizziness;

The man who stuffed him don't half know his
business!''
And the barber kept on shaving. . . .

''With some sawdust and bark
I could stuff in the dark
An owl better than that.
I could make an old bat
Look more like an owl
Than that horrid fowl,
Stuck up there so stiff like a side of coarse
leather;
In fact, about him there's not one natural
feather.''

Just then with a wink and a sly normal lurch,
The owl, very gravely, got down from his perch,
Walked round, and regarded his fault-finding
critic,
(Who thought he was stuffed) with a glance
analytic,
And then fairly hooted, as if he should say:
''Your learning's at fault, this time, anyway;
Don't waste it again on a live bird, I pray.
I'm an owl; you're another. Sir Critic,
good-day!''
And the barber kept on shaving.

(In Hazel Felleman, sel., *The Best Loved Poems of
the American People* [Garden City, New York:
Doubleday, 1936], pp. 496–97.)

Someone has said: ''If they gave rewards for finding fault, some people would get rich quick.''
The best weapon against cynicism and negative
thinking is a positive mental attitude. Remember the
story of the snail and the cherry tree.
One raw, windy day a snail started to climb a

cherry tree. Some birds in a neighboring tree chat-
tered their ridicule.

"Hey, you dumb snail, where do you think you're
going?" said one of them. "Why are you climbing
that tree? There are no cherries on it!"

"There will be when I get there," said the snail.

Or, recall with me the Monday morning a young
woman got on the elevator, humming cheerfully.

"What have you got to be so happy about today?"
inquired the office grouch.

"I never lived this day before!" was her reply.

Then there was the little six-year-old girl who is
destined to succeed. She visited a farm one day,
wanting to buy a large watermelon. "That's three
dollars," said the farmer. "I've only got thirty
cents," said the little girl. The farmer pointed to a
very small watermelon in the field and said, "How
about that one?" "Okay, I'll take it," said the little
girl. "But leave it on the vine. I'll be back for it in a
month."

I'll never forget a choice friend who was somewhat older in years but young in spirit. Although
mostly bedridden, she got around in a wheelchair
and was a real dynamo. She had a small business that
she conducted from her apartment, she served on
many committees and regularly helped charitable
causes in many capacities.

One day a new acquaintance asked her how she
had come to be in the wheelchair.

"Infantile paralysis," she replied. "In the beginning, I was almost completely paralyzed."

"It's obviously still a serious handicap," said the
acquaintance. "How do you cope? How do you do all
the things you do?"

"Ah!" said she with a smile. "The paralysis never
touched my heart or my head."

What would life be if we had no courage to attempt anything?

Consider the story of the chicken farmer whose land was flooded virtually every spring. He didn't want to move, but when the waters backed up onto his land and flooded his chicken coops, he was always faced with the problem of moving the chickens to higher ground. Some years he couldn't move them all in time, and hundreds of chickens drowned.

One year after a particularly bad flood, he had very heavy losses. He came into the farmhouse and, in a voice filled with despair, said to his wife, "I've had it. We can't afford to buy another place. We couldn't even sell this one. I don't know what to do!"

His wife saw an opportunity in the midst of their adversity. "Raise ducks," she said.

Consider the wisdom of Rudyard Kipling: "We have forty million reasons for failure, but not a single excuse."

Why do some people succeed while others do not? In the simplest terms, successful people act and others don't. Successful people are doers. Even if they just stare out the window, most of them are constantly thinking of new and better ways to perform. They have initiative, and that's what the world pays for in money and honor. Success comes from thinking positive, and then doing something about it. An unidentified author wrote:

> Remember this your lifetime through—
> Tomorrow, there will be more to do . . .
> And failure waits for all who stay
> With some success made yesterday . . .
> Tomorrow, you must try once more
> And even harder than before.

PART I

Knowing

Chapter 2

Prayer— the Simplest Form of Speech

Have you ever had the desire to have an audience with God? "May I have five minutes, please? I have some things stored up to say, some burdens that I've carried that I'd like to unload, some direction, pure intelligence, that I'd like to receive on what I'm supposed to do next in life. It wouldn't take long, my audience with God. Isn't there time for me?"

Sometimes there's the feeling that our Father doesn't have time for us. We pray and don't feel His answer. We hear our own pleading words loud in our heads and nothing else. Finally, we say to ourselves, "Maybe there are too many voices praying right now and He can't hear me. Maybe I didn't pray long enough. Maybe I wasn't good enough." But all the time our hearts are crying for our Father to be near. Where is He?

I love the experience someone related of the little
boy who was asked a similar question and who gave
a profound answer:

He was just a little lad
And on that Sabbath day
Was walking home from Sunday School
And dawdling on the way.

He scuffed his foot upon the grass
And saw a caterpillar;
He picked a fluffy milkweed pod,
And blew out all the filler.

A bird's nest in the tree o'er head
So wisely placed and high
Was just another wonder
That caught his eager eye.

A neighbor watched his zig-zag path
And hailed him from the lawn,
And he asked him where he'd been that day
And what was going on.

"I've been to Sunday School," he said,
And just beside the trail
He stooped and turned the sod, and there
He found a little snail.

"Ah, a fine way," the neighbor said,
"For a boy to spend his time.
If you can tell me where God is,
I'll give you a brand new dime."

Quick as a flash his answer came,
Nor were his accents faint—
"I'll give you a dollar, mister,
If you can tell me where God ain't."

This little boy has the answer, all right. No matter where any of us is, we can be with God. He can hear our voices. We can feel His Spirit and be comforted. Years ago I read the following experience of a little girl at a coffee shop:

"The lunch counter had that stainless steel and nickel shine indigenous to lunch counters—and in the soft early morning light it looked clean and impersonal but sort of cheerful.

"Twenty-odd citizens were lined up on the stools. There were college students, a somber-looking man with a briefcase, two young nurses, a little rumpled and hollow-eyed after a night on duty at the nearby hospital, a family with a little girl, and a sullen teenager impartially distributing lipstick between her mouth and her breakfast.

"The lunchroom was quiet except for the occasional sharp crack of an eggshell in the counterman's expert hand, the sputter of frying bacon, and the bored voice of a customer, ordering more food.

"The customers were engrossed in their own thoughts—inconspicuous, anonymous, brought together by nothing more binding than the tribal custom of eating in the morning. They did not even have real hunger in common . . . just eating because people do.

"And then at the end of the counter the little girl said in a carrying voice, 'Mother, don't we ask the blessing here?'

"The counterman stopped wiping the already spotless counter and grinned at her suddenly.

" 'Sure we do, sister,' he said. 'You say it.'

"She bowed her smooth little head. The young counterman turned and glanced firmly at his customers and bowed his head, too. Up and down the counter heads went down, the nurses, the students, and the man with the briefcase, and then, slowly, the teenager.

"The breathless little voice was loud in the room:

" 'Our Heavenly Father, we thank thee for our lives and for our blessings. By thy hand are we fed, and by thy hand we receive our daily bread. Amen.'

"Heads went up along the counter. Eating was resumed but somehow the atmosphere had subtly changed. The man with the briefcase smiled and remarked to the nurses that he had a new baby in their hospital. Conversation became general.

"The counterman smiled at the students and said, 'Well, I won't be seeing you after this week. I reckon I'm going to Korea.' They paused, paying their check, to talk with him about it. Somehow a tenuous bond of friendliness and mutual confidence had grown up in the room, and the little girl, oblivious to what she had done, lathered her waffle with syrup and ate it happily."

It was Conrad Hilton, the head of a vast hotel chain, who was touched by a letter from a twelve-year-old boy, a letter which in turn had a great effect on America. Here is the story in his own words:

"Early Thursday morning on February 5, 1953, a car pulled away from the White House and the President of the United States directed the driver—*to go to a prayer meeting.*

"I was on hand to see President Eisenhower, Justices of the Supreme Court, Senators, Congressmen, bow their heads together in prayer at that breakfast. I saw protocol swept aside and Vice President Nixon, Chief Justice Vinson, diplomats, drop into any empty seat among the 500 guests.

"To be host to such a gathering was a great honor for me. To see the enlarged picture of Uncle Sam [shown on his knees] dominate the Mayflower Hotel ballroom, to hear that room hushed in prayer—it all seemed like a miracle.

"Sitting there, I thought back to the day, two years ago, when a letter came to my office, a small envelope nearly lost in a stack of mail. Yet of all the letters that arrived that day this small unassuming note about a speech I had made was the most important: " 'Dear Mr. Hilton:

" 'I have read your talk in the *Herald Tribune*, and I think it was wonderful. Especially that our faith in God was our only hope. You are very right and I think if everyone would fall down and pray we would have real peace. Sincerely yours, Daniel Paolucci.

" 'P.S. I am a boy of 12. May I please have an answer?'

"If young Daniel knew what it did to the heart of a man to find that a few of what he often feels are many repetitious words have fallen on listening ears, he would understand how grateful I was.

"Automatically, I did the conventional thing. I wrote Daniel a grateful reply, enclosing a copy of the address he had liked. But I couldn't shake off his P.S.: 'May I please have an answer?'

"I read the clipping in the *Herald Tribune*: '. . . in our struggle for freedom our greatest weapon will be our love of, and our faith in God.' It dawned on me that something was lacking in that speech. Something that had been in Daniel's letter. Funny that I, who have known prayer and trusted the power of prayer all my life, should not have mentioned it.

"It was on a train to Chicago that, mentally, I first saw Uncle Sam on his knees praying. Praying for what? Certainly not: 'That God be on my side.' Through two ghastly wars both sides made that prayer and it didn't get much peace even for the victor. Obviously, that hasn't worked. Daniel himself must have learned how foolish it would be to explain to his Algebra teacher how *he'd* like mathematics to work.

'' 'That I be on God's side.' That would be Uncle Sam's peace prayer.

"Still fired with this concept when the train pulled into Chicago, I bought a daily paper. The first thing that caught my eye was a cartoon entitled: 'When Problems Overwhelm.' Before a littered desk sat the figure of Uncle Sam, harassed by troubles. But he didn't look like the Uncle Sam I had visualized on the train: Strong, earnest, grounded on a rock of faith. Here sat the harassed old fellow. And from the wall an infinitely compassionate portrait of Abraham Lincoln spoke: 'Have you tried prayer, Sam?'

"To me it was the confirmation of my vision. Back in New York I talked it over with Dr. Norman Vincent Peale and my devoted friend, the late Fulton Oursler, both of whom encouraged me to proceed. In the spirit of humility and with loving advice a prayer took form.

"Next came the idea for a pictorial presentation of the prayer—to be ready for publication in national magazines on Uncle Sam's birthday, July 4th, two months off.

"Time was short. Where was the artist who could paint Uncle Sam? Paint him as he must be . . . not weak, not knocked to his knees, but freely, confidently, knowing how to do battle for peace.

"Two of the greatest American artists were approached. They were enthusiastic, but their work schedule would not permit them to start immediately.

"When a former secretary of mine, who had turned to painting, asked if she might try, I shrugged her off. Only a very great artist could do justice to the theme. But I wasn't reckoning with the power of prayer . . . one fruit of which is inspiration.

"Several days later she handed me her work. I couldn't believe it. Here was the Uncle Sam I had seen on the train.

"When I showed it to a Jesuit Father who knew her earlier works, he said simply, 'She has painted better than she knows.'

"Within the first 5 days after 'America on its Knees' appeared in national magazines, 5,000 people had written for 27,000 copies. Among them were hundreds of letters from children and teenagers.

"That was just the beginning of the snowball. Since then we have distributed 300,000 copies throughout the world. . . .

"Here was the idea and how it grew. And I sat there that morning, in the Mayflower Hotel, seeing this event—the President, the Cabinet, Uncle Sam praying at the start of a new administration.

" 'Prayer today is a necessity,' President Eisenhower stated when he arose to speak. 'We know that our prayers may be imperfect . . . We are imperfect human beings. But if we can make the effort, then there is something that ties us all together.'

"Just prior to this I greeted the assemblage as proud host and then read the Uncle Sam prayer . . . The President of the United States, the Vice President, Cabinet, Justices, diplomats, top American leaders listened to the words below, which had been inspired by 12-year-old Daniel Paolucci . . .

OUR FATHER IN HEAVEN:

"We pray that You save us from ourselves.

"The world that You have made for us, to live in

peace, we have made into an armed camp. We live in fear of war to come.

"We are afraid of 'the terror that flies by night, and the arrow that flies by day, the pestilence that walks in darkness and the destruction that wastes at noonday.'

"We have turned from You to go our selfish way. We have broken Your commandments and denied Your truth. We have left Your altars to serve the false gods of money and pleasure and power. Forgive us and help us.

"Now, darkness gathers around us and we are confused in all our counsels. Losing faith in You, we lose faith in ourselves.

"Inspire us with wisdom, all of us, of every color, race and creed, to use our wealth, our strength, to help our brother, instead of destroying him.

"Help us to do Your will as it is done in heaven and to be worthy of Your promise of peace on earth.

"Fill us with new faith, new strength, and new courage, that we may win the battle for peace.

"Be swift to save us, dear God, before the darkness falls." ("What Is . . . Uncle Sam's Prayer?" *Guideposts*, July 1953, pp. 1-4. Reprinted with permission from Guideposts Magazine. Copyright © 1953 by Guideposts Associates, Inc., Carmel, NY 10512.)

The little boy who was on his way home from Sunday School, the little girl in the coffee shop, and the great hotel owner and executive all learned how God, the Father, is as close to us as a prayer. Even when it seems we don't feel Him, He is not removed.

In my own experience the deepest feelings of mankind were summed up as I listened to the words of a young, mentally handicapped boy who was called on to give his first public prayer in an LDS meeting. He, too, was only twelve years old and was not a member of the Church. He said, simply:

Heavenly Father, this is Michael speaking to you.
Sometimes you seem far away,
And sometimes you seem close in.
This morning please be close in.
This is Michael saying, Amen.

The whole of the human race (all five-plus billion of us) are children of a divine Father. He knows us. He loves us. And He stands ready to touch and inspire us through prayer and private communication if we will but seek.

Chapter 3

Love Signs

Every few years many of us have the challenge and experience of renewing our driver's licenses. Where I live it is mandatory that the driver pass a written test which includes knowing the meaning and color of road signs.

These signs are posted to give us instruction. We've seen them everywhere. We recognize what they mean even before we can read them. What's the red sign with eight sides? A stop sign, of course. The triangle is a yield sign. And the square, green sign tells us where the road goes. It's simple and easy to understand. No questions needed. These days we even have international signs which are illustrated so there will be no mistake regardless of our culture or language. The signs are standard.

But there are some signs in life that aren't standard at all. Those are the signs that say, "I love you." They are the signs that one person gives another to say, "You matter to me." "You're something special." "You have worth and are important in my eyes." And they're the signs we all seek in life. Mom looks for them from Dad, and he looks for them from her. The children need them from their parents. We all need them from each other. Oliver Wendell Holmes reminds us:

> Oh, there be many things
> That seem right fair, below, above;
> But sure not one among them all
> Is half so sweet as love.

Yes, it's true that love signs, unlike street signs, are not standard. Nobody gives them in quite the same way. The way I express my love to my fellowmen may not be the way you express your love to them. That which means "I love you" to me may not mean that at all to you. Because the signs are so different, it is easy to be confused about what others mean.

One woman related that when she was angry or sad, she liked nothing better than to have her husband come and talk to her and pat her and tell her that everything was all right. She liked to be told, in effect, "There, there. You're OK."

But her husband was just the opposite. When he was angry or sad, he wanted only one thing—to be left alone. All alone. Can you foresee the trouble? Every time he was upset, she would come running to him with pats and hugs and comforting words. It certainly seemed the right thing to do. It was just what she would want in a similar situation. But as for him

—he couldn't handle it. All he wanted in the world when he was upset was to be as far away as possible.

As for her, when she was feeling low, oh, how she wanted him to come to her—and he never did! He left her alone, just as he would have wanted had he been in her shoes. She couldn't believe his insensitivity.

What's obvious here is that neither understood a simple principle. Love means different things to different people. "I can tell you love me," says one, "because you leave me alone when I'm sad." "I can tell you love me," says another, "because you don't leave me alone when I'm sad." Ironic as it may be, we often show our love to others just the way we would want them to show it to us. But sometimes that's not the right way to go about it at all.

How many wives are longing for a bouquet of flowers or a compliment on their appearance from their husbands? How many husbands already think they are showing their love by mowing the lawn well and taking out the garbage without being asked?

Not stopping to ask ourselves what it is that really means love to the other person is as crazy as the teenage boy who gave his mother a hard-rock album for Christmas. It was, after all, just what he wanted. If somebody had given it to him, he would have thought that person really loved him. But his mother? Well, she graciously thanked him and then stored it with *his* hard-rock albums.

In a certain city there was an obstetrician whom some expectant mothers avoided. Apparently he was gruff in his manner and brief with his words. He didn't have a warm bedside manner and didn't know how to show concern for his patients. But those who did go to him for medical assistance said he showed his concern in another way—maybe even a more important way. He took meticulous care of their health. He was far more thorough than most of the doctors in his city.

Yes, we show our love for each other in different ways, and maybe sometimes when we are feeling un- loved by our family members or our marriage part- ner, it is just because we aren't speaking the same language. They are showing their love for us in one way—while we were really hoping for another. A sign of true love is when two people say to each other with their eyes, "You don't have to be on guard with me."

Lael J. Littke tells of an experience from her youth that taught her something about love and its signs:

"Mother was lying pale and quiet on the high hos- pital bed when Dad and I entered the room. It frightened me to see her that way, so to hide my emo- tions I loped to her side greeting her with the raucous 'HIYA' I used for my thirteen-year-old girlfriends. She smiled at me and asked how I was and how the other children were. Fine, I assured her, except for Tootie's chicken pox, which Mrs. Donegan next door claimed looked more like smallpox to her, and Tom's mashed finger which was the only thing that got hurt when the tractor ran away with him. Fine, I told her again, except that things just didn't go right and the house was empty without her, and I was a miserable substitute for her, and we missed her desperately, and, as a matter of fact, everything was just terrible. I broke down and cried on her crisp white sheet. She smoothed my hair and told me to sit down in the chair nearby.

"My father approached the bed then, and through my sniffles and sobs I watched with interest. In the stories I had read, a husband visiting his wife in the hospital always rushed to her bedside and buried his face in her neck, all the while murmuring things like, 'My darling, I can't stand to see you this way.'

"My father was big and never said much, but in the stories it was always the strong, silent ones who were the most romantic. At home Dad was undemonstrative, but this was a different situation, wasn't it?

"Slowly Dad approached the bed. He stood there a moment, fiddling with the glass tube in the water container on the small table. Then he looked straight at mother. He cleared his throat.

" 'The jersey had her calf last night,' he said. He shifted his weight. 'Got nearly 300 eggs from the old hens.'

"I could scarcely believe my ears. This is marriage? I thought. For this someday I will get married so that my husband can come to my hospital bedside and tell me some cow has had a calf? A wave of pity washed over me, pity for my mother tied all these years to a man whose main interests were in how many eggs the hens had laid.

"I stood up and opened my mouth to tell my mother something—anything—which would make her understand that Dad missed her, too. Before I could blurt out anything, my glance snagged on Dad's face. There were tears in his eyes. He was looking down at mother. A peek at my mother's face told me she understood perfectly what he was trying to convey to her. She smiled up at him and he touched her cheek with his rough . . . farmer's hand.

"I didn't see deep into their souls with a sudden flash of perception as the people did in the magazine stories, but I saw enough to make me begin to understand a little about a different kind of love. There were no violins sobbing out romantic melodies, but somewhere, beyond my hearing, there were angels singing of a plain and humble love which was deep enough, big enough, strong enough, to last throughout eternity.'' (''No Violins,'' *Relief Society Magazine,* April 1966, pp. 299–300.)

Well, people, even people close to us, don't always give us love quite in the ways we might order it. But we still have to recognize it for what it is. Love may be packaged differently than we might hope, but it is love all the same. Instead of lamenting that we miss the pats or the solitude, instead of hoping for the words when the words don't come easily, let us just teach ourselves to recognize the love signs, however they come. And beyond that, if we are really wise, let us learn to understand our partners and family members well enough to give them the kind of love signs they need, instead of the kind *we think* they need.

Chapter 4

Creating
Memories

Have you ever stopped at the end of a special day and said to yourself, ''I'll never forget this day as long as I live''? You know what? In most instances you'll forget it. In a world where most of us can't remember what we did yesterday, it's almost certain that we won't remember last year or last decade or the day we thought so memorable. Oh, broad outlines may remain in our minds, but the details—the sights and sounds, the feelings that made it special—will fade forever. No doubt you've seen it happen in your own life. You run into an old acquaintance and can't recall his name. You're talking with old friends about a shared experience, and they're citing moments you can't remember.

The fact is, all the momentous times of your life will vanish from you if you don't find a way to capture them. And the best way of doing that may be the oldest way—keeping a record. You may just want to write occasionally, or you might want to keep a more detailed record daily or weekly. But there is nothing that will bring you more enduring pleasure than keeping and reading again the record of your triumphs and pleasures, your heartaches and growth.

Writer Norman M. Lobsenz described an interesting experience regarding record keeping: "I was complaining to my wife that our teenage children seemed so caught up in themselves, so egocentrically unaware of the world around them, that I wondered if they would *ever* grow up. For answer, my wife dug into an old carton and took out a yellowing diary of her own. The date on the cover was 1945, when she was in her early teens. 'Listen to this,' she said. 'May 7—Terrible time in school, flunked math quiz. Nancy bragged about her new bike. Why can't I have one? . . . I am bored, *bored*, BORED. Nothing important ever happens. Oh yes, P.S.—Today's V-E Day. The war is over in Europe.' " ("New Ways to Capture Memories," *Reader's Digest*, November 1975, p. 180.)

When you keep a journal, you learn that no life is dull, especially yours. Many complain that they can't keep a journal because nothing happens to them, but is that true? Even a description of the lowliest events can take on importance later. Listen to how quaint this 1970 journal entry sounds talking about typical shopping prices of the day. It reads: "Eggs down to 41 cents this week from 53 a few weeks ago. Gas up to 35 cents from 26.9 a month ago" (in William G. Hartley, "Diary and Journal Ideas," *New Era*, March 1977, pp. 42–43).

The point is, your life is unlike any other and it deserves recording. President Spencer W. Kimball said: "You are unique, and there may be incidents in your experience that are more noble and praiseworthy in their way than those recorded in any other life. There may be a flash of illumination here and a story of faithfulness there; you should truthfully record your real self and not what other people may see in you." (Quoted in "Diary and Journal Ideas," p. 42.)

And one of the greatest values of a journal is that it gives you a bit of immortality. We live in a world where many don't even know their own parents and grandparents. Oh, they may think they do, but most of us miss knowing from the inside who our parents were, what they dreamed and what they feared. Do you not want your children and grandchildren to know you?

Several years ago I approached my wife and said, "Let's create some special memories for our daughters, their partners, and our two mothers [both of whom were widowed at the time]." She said, "What do you mean?" I said, "I have several assignments in Europe coming up, and just think of the memories we could create if we took our family with us." Her quick response was, "We can't afford it." I said, "Let's take our savings and share the learning experience with our loved ones, and on our way home we will visit the Holy Land at Christmastime." There are not words and space enough to record here the experience of a lifetime we shared together. Spiritually, culturally, and educationally, memories were made for eternity. One of our daughters recorded in detail the events, our feelings and expressions that have now been passed along to the next generation!

One of the most heartwarming stories I've ever heard would have been lost to the world if Les Goates hadn't been reviewing his life and decided to record it. He said that he would never forget the autumn of 1918, "that terribly climactic year of World War I during which more than 14 million people died of that awful scourge 'the black plague,' or Spanish influenza.

"Winter came early that year and froze much of the sugar beet crop in the ground. My dad and brother Francis were desperately trying to get out of the frosty ground one load of beets each day which they would plow out of the ground, cut off the tops, and toss the beets, one at a time, into the huge red beet wagon and then haul the load off to the sugar factory. It was slow and tedious work due to the frost and the lack of farm help, since my brother Floyd and I were in the army and Francis, or Franz, as everybody called him, was too young for the military service.

"While they were thusly engaged in harvesting the family's only cash crop and were having their evening meal one day, a phone call came through from our elder brother, George Albert, . . . bearing the tragic news that Kenneth, nine-year-old son of our brother Charles, . . . had been stricken with the dread 'flu,' and after only a few hours of violent sickness, had died on his father's lap; and would dad please come . . . and bring the boy home and lay him away in the family plot. . . .

"My father cranked up his old flap-curtained Chevrolet and headed [north] to bring his little grandson home for burial. When he arrived at the home he found 'Charl' sprawled across the cold form of his dear one, the ugly brown discharge of the black plague oozing from his ears and nose and virtually burning up with fever.

" 'Take my boy home,' muttered the stricken young father, 'and lay him away in the family lot and come back for me tomorrow.' "

Within one week Les's father made four separate trips in the old Chevrolet, bringing home for burial his son and three grandchildren, all who had died of the terrible flu.

Then, on the seventh day of the ordeal, according to Les's account, "dad said to Franz, 'Well, son, we had better get down to the field and see if we can get another load of beets out of the ground before they get frozen in any tighter. Hitch up and let's be on our way.'

". . . As they drove along the Saratoga Road, they passed wagon after wagon-load of beets being hauled to the factory and driven by neighborhood farmers. As they passed by, each driver would wave a greeting: 'Hi ya, Uncle George,' 'Sure sorry, George,' 'Tough break, George,' 'You've got a lot of friends, George.'

"On the last wagon was the town comedian, freckled-faced Jasper Rolfe. He waved a cheery greeting and called out: 'That's all of 'em, Uncle George.'

"My dad turned to Francis and said: 'I wish it was all of ours.'

"When they arrived at the farm gate, Francis jumped down off the big red beet wagon and opened the gate as we drove onto the field. He pulled up, stopped the team, paused a moment and scanned the field, from left to right and back and forth—and lo and behold, there wasn't a sugar beet on the whole field. Then it dawned upon him what Jasper Rolfe meant when he called out: 'That's all of 'em, Uncle George!' . . .

"Then father sat down on a pile of beet tops—this man who brought four of his loved ones home for burial in the course of only six days; made caskets, dug graves, and even helped with the burial clothing

—this amazing man who never faltered, nor flinched, nor wavered throughout this agonizing ordeal—sat down on a pile of beet tops and sobbed like a little child." (Quoted in Vaughn J. Featherstone, " 'Now Abideth Faith, Hope, and Charity,' " *Ensign*, July 1973, pp. 36-37.)

Now, if Les Goates hadn't decided to record his life and the events that closely touched it, we would have lost forever this story of his father and the beets. Your life has moments like that that deserve recording—moments that may have happened to no one else. Start today to write them down. Your posterity deserves to know you.

Chapter 5

Boundaries, Rules, and Blessings

One writer wrote some rules that are guaranteed to work to raise children even when all else fails. He calls them the art of strategic retreat. You try number one rule and if it doesn't work, try number two, and when it doesn't work, you try number three, and so forth. Let me share some of them with you for those times when all your best parenting tricks have failed. Here, for example, are his rules for bedtime:

1. Bedtime for children is eight o'clock sharp! There'll be no discussion on the matter. Now, if that doesn't work there's always rule number two.

2. Tonight only, bedtime will be not one minute past 8:30. Now, if that doesn't work there is always rule number three. (Notice how it very subtly includes a treat.)

3. Children who fall asleep while staying up late will not be carried to bed.

4. Unless they won't wake up.

Identify with that, desperate parents? You remember when you were a child. You did everything you were told—and did it immediately. But these kids today . . . !

Here are his rules on mealtime:

1. Children must clean their plates.

2. No dessert for children who don't.

3. Absolutely *no second dessert.*

Parents everywhere are retreating from their rules. They question them; they question their right to set them; they're afraid to stick to them once they're set. Sometimes the consequences of enforcing a family rule seem too unbearable. The mother says, "No ice-cream cone," as they pass the tempting counter—and suddenly she has on her hands a toddler with a tantrum. The father tells his teenager who stayed out too late that he can't use the car for a week, but one day later he's not in the mood to enforce his own dictate.

Family rules become fluid and eventually meaningless. And parents everywhere wonder why their children don't understand the meaning of boundaries. There are few things more difficult than the art of making a rule agreeable. One day a young teenager I was counseling said to me: "The rules and advice my parents give would be more acceptable if they didn't always conflict with my plans."

Les Johnson wrote of the following experience: "On the farm where I spent my youth, I noticed that the first thing that the cattle did when they were let out in the spring was to head for the nearest fence. They leaned on it, marched along it, crawled through it, or jumped over it. There was no apparent reason for their action since the other side of the fence was summer fallow—sandy, dry, undigestible summer fallow.''

It seems even cows have a need to explore. ''They wanted to find out as quickly as they could just how far they could go,'' continues Johnson. What were the limits of their ''newfound freedom'' after the confinement of winter?

And people, especially young people, are much the same. They want to find out what their limits are. As Johnson wrote: ''Cattle will not prosper if they spend their time crawling through a fence or unhappily staring down at dusty summer fallow. They will be as unhappy as the child who can't find the borders of his existence.''

There is no more miserable person than he who has no boundaries on his behavior. He is insecure; he does not know who he is or what is expected of him. There is, surprisingly enough, great relief and freedom in knowing, as Les Johnson put it, ''This, this, and this I can do—But that I cannot do!'' (''Looking for a Fence,'' *Scouting*, December 1964, p. 14.)

Those who have visited Yellowstone National Park will have noticed that there are boardwalks around the hot pools which bubble up from beneath the earth's surface. Stationed along these walks are signs which say quite distinctly, ''Do not get off the path.'' Why? Are the park officials trying to limit in some malignant way the freedom of those who would enjoy the pools? Obviously not. They know that should someone stumble into them or tread upon a soft spot near them, injury would be inevitable. The pools are so hot that a person's skin would fry and scar. Some unwary trespasser off the path could even die. Everyone with sense applauds the signs that say, ''Do not get off the path.'' I'll always appreciate the sign posted on a beautiful lawn at a national monument which said: "Keep off. Your feet are killing me." An old New England seaman once said to me: "When a man does not know what harbor he is making for, no wind is the right wind."

Now, as parents who want fervently for our children to grow up into honest, responsible, and happy human beings, let us be unafraid to establish rules of conduct for our children. We are not doing them any favor if we adopt an "anything goes" attitude toward them. We're not helping them if, under pressure, we retreat from our word.

It is important that you sit down with your children and tell them what you expect of them. Parents who have tried this and enlisted their children's suggestions are surprised how sensible their children really are. When asked, they can come up with some good rules for themselves. Let them help you. Rules that are mutually agreed upon are much easier to enforce than parental dictates.

And as you create your family rules, the boundaries beyond which your children may not tread, consider that a fence that is too tight will constrict and cause rebellion, while a fence that is too loose will leave them wandering and insecure.

Now, Les Johnson noted that, after his father electrified the fence, in a few days the cattle herd "knew where the fence was and they stayed away from it. They grazed contentedly," he continues, "and became fat and healthy. At the time it seemed to me to be a waste of power to leave the charger running when no animal came near it. My father shut it off and set me to watch.

"Within an hour a steer came up to test the fence. He was looking for security. There was no shock. He looked back at the herd. He was confused. He jumped the fence. Had I not been there, others would have soon followed." ("Looking for a Fence," pp. 14–15.)

And children are the same. Even after your rules are firmly established and mutually agreed upon, they will test you to see if the rules hold. Too often they don't. It is difficult to be consistent as a parent. It takes energy and determination to stick to your guns and mean what you say. But if you are inconsistent, your children will believe that your word is always open for debate. They will fight you and test you and knock heads until you are both losers.

One of the Lord's great strengths is his consistency. While the world may clamor today that nothing is either good or bad in itself, the Lord tells us something different. There is a right and a wrong. There are fences beyond which we may not go without serious consequences to our own happiness. He has given us the perfect example of parenting. He has laid out the laws for his children so we clearly understand them. And he has even gone a step further. He has said that if we obey his law, he will bless us. He is bound to do so.

The scriptures say it this way: "There is a law, irrevocably decreed in heaven before the foundations of this world, upon which all blessings are predicated—and when we obtain any blessing from God, it is by obedience to that law upon which it is predicated" (D&C 130:20–21).

With the Lord there is no strategic retreat. He is not too lazy or indifferent to enforce His commandments. As unpopular to us as it may be to be forthright these days, the Lord means what He says.

May I leave with you the prayer that as a parent you may have the courage to give your children guidelines to live by, and that as a child of an Eternal Father in Heaven you may be just as diligent in following His laws.

Chapter 6

Declare Your Own Independence

Many years ago our forefathers declared their independence from England. Ever since, it seems that there has been a constant struggle within each of us to declare our own independence.

Do you ever have the feeling you would like to do something really wonderful with your life, that there is a sleeping giant within you just waiting to be aroused? We want to be great—and we would be, we think, if life didn't shackle us in so many ways. We think, "I could be great, I really could, but this or that stands in my way."

Every July Fourth we think back to the Declaration of Independence, the document that declared all men free—but many of us don't feel free. Our lives often seem out of control, raging beyond us. Tomorrow, we think, tomorrow we'll get beyond this pressure or that habit that is holding us back.

But, you know, there's only one thing holding you back in life—you. You shackle yourself, keep yourself tied down beneath your dreams. If you're not getting what you want in life, it is simply because you don't want it badly enough.

Let me give you an example. I know a young man who has put on a little bit of weight. He thinks he wants nothing so much in the world as to be trim and attractive again. He talks about it all the time—hates himself for his extra pounds. He avoids the bathroom scale. (It is a little like the fellow who got on one of those weighing machines that stamp out one's weight on a card. When the card came out it said, "Come back in ten minutes—alone!") But there is something in life he wants more than a trim body— whatever is in the refrigerator. He desires that extra piece of pecan pie with whipped cream or the raspberry sundae—or whatever—more than any weight loss, and he's only fooling himself not to admit it.

Another example. Many of us would like to get up just a bit earlier every morning, would like that extra minute in the morning to exercise or compose ourselves or just plan the day. But then the morning comes and our desires change. The mattress is so compelling that the extra minute loses in the race. We didn't want that extra time nearly as much as we thought we did.

All of us, it seems, have inclinations that pull us in opposite directions. And when our desires are at war, one with another, it is well for us to stop and ponder what it is we really want. It is time for us to master our warring desires into a pattern of behavior that will lead us to our goals. As we read in Proverbs, "He that ruleth his spirit [is mightier] than he that taketh a city'' (Proverbs 16:32).

And most of the world's great thinkers have had similar thoughts as they have reflected on their achievements.

Seneca: ''Most powerful is he who has himself in his own power.''

Cicero: ''Control thyself.''

Da Vinci: ''You will never have a greater or lesser dominion than that over yourself.''

Plato: ''The first and best victory is to conquer self.''

And it seems that the reason why the first victory is the one over self is that all others are impossible until that is achieved. We must be able to act out in the hurried moments of our lives those things we really want when we have time to think about them. Our dreams are not impossible. Each of us has more latent power than we realize. We just need to harness our desires and make them work for us rather than against us. My mother often said: ''Don't let the fact that you can't do all you want to do keep you from doing what you can do.''

Ralph Waldo Emerson summed up the method for making it work. He said, ''Do the thing and you will have the power; but they that do not the thing have not the power.'' Or, stated a different way—Be bigger than anything that can happen to you.

The answer, then, is simple. It is only when we actually begin to pursue our dream that we find we have the power and the talent to carry it off. While we sit wondering and placating ourselves with momentary pleasures nothing ever happens. The point is to begin and let the thrill of success give us the impetus to move forward.

I know a young woman who wanted desperately to master a certain area of her life. She wanted to develop the habit of daily scripture reading, adding spiritual insight to her days and her life. But the task seemed impossible. She had a million excuses why she just couldn't do it, making lots of false starts without following through. Then finally she decided to keep a personal record of how many consecutive days she could read without missing. She decided that if she did miss a day, she would have to start over on her count.

Well, when she finally got started on her scripture reading plan, her real desire for spiritual insight took hold. Those few moments reading became for her the most precious of the day. The consecutive days she went without missing her reading grew from ten to twenty to three hundred. No matter how tired she was or how full her day, no passing fancy was stronger for her than the deeper desire to sit down and spend some time with the Lord's word. That's taking hold of your life. What would life be if we had no courage to attempt anything?

It is just as easy, after all, to let your higher desires rule your life as it is to allow your lower ones to do so. It's all a matter of habit.

In this regard, consider the following: ''Out in Wyoming, near Guernsey, one can see ruts several feet deep in solid stone cut by the covered wagons of the westbound pioneers of more than a century ago. One contemplates the first covered wagon that came that way. He did not know which way to travel—except to follow the setting sun. But the driver of the second wagon must have been encouraged when he found that he could follow the ever so faint tracks of the first pioneer. And for the third, and fourth, and fifth wagon driver, the trail was a little better. Year after year, until the railroad was completed in 1869, more covered wagons followed that trail until ruts were cut deep into solid rock.

"Actions and habits are like that, too. . . . The first act leaves an ever so faint mark on a person. But it makes it easier for a second act to follow the trail left by the first one. And a third, and a fourth, and a fifth. Soon that trail is cut into the solid rock of that person's character. And he has a habit formed, for good or bad." (As found in Albert L. Zobell, Jr., comp., *Story Lore* [Salt Lake City: Bookcraft, 1956], pp. 66–67.)

In a related vein William James said: "'We are spinning our own fates, good or evil, and never to be undone. Every smallest stroke of virtue or of vice leaves its never so little scar. The drunken Rip Van Winkle, in Jefferson's play, excuses himself for every fresh dereliction by saying, 'I won't count this time!' Well! he may not count it, . . . but it is being counted nonetheless. Down among his nerve-cells and fibres the molecules are counting it, registering and storing it up to be used against him when the next temptation comes. Nothing we ever do is, in strict scientific literalness, wiped out. Of course, this has its good side as well as its bad one. As we become permanent drunkards by so many separate drinks, so we become saints in the moral, and authorities and experts in the practical and scientific spheres, by so many separate acts and hours of work." (*The Principles of Psychology* [1890; reprint, Cambridge: Harvard University Press, 1983], pp. 130–31.)

So it seems the greatest challenge is in just beginning to implement your highest self, your best desires. That first path through the wilderness is the only uncharted one. After that, the way becomes easier and easier. Self-mastery is not as difficult as the initial steps in that direction make you believe some-times.

Whenever we think about the Declaration of Independence, let's make our own declaration. Declare yourself free of the bad habits and passing pleasures that are barring you from your dreams.

The greatest waste of our natural resources is the number of people who never achieve their potential. Remember it is never too late to be what you might have been.

Chapter 7

Your Control Center

Those of us who understand a little about the space age know what a mission control center is. It is that complex of screens and computers and dials and knobs that launches a craft out into space and helps to control and monitor it while it's in flight. And we know what the control center of an airplane is. It's that sophisticated board of instruments that controls the dip, the angle, the height, and the speed of a steel bird while it flies through space. Even electrical generating plants have their control centers where skilled engineers can turn on or shut off the operation at will. Control centers. Just thinking about them brings up a question that each of us might well ask himself: "Where is my personal control center?"

The popular newspaper columnist Sydney J. Harris, as he told the story in an article appearing in the *Chicago Daily News,* walked one night with a friend to a newsstand. The friend bought a paper and thanked the newsboy politely, but the newsboy didn't even acknowledge the courtesy.

"A sullen fellow, isn't he?" Harris commented.

"Oh, he's that way every night," shrugged his friend.

"Then why do you continue to be so polite to him?" Harris asked.

"Why not?" inquired the friend. "Why should I let him decide how I'm going to act?"

That's an intriguing thought. Each of us every day has the opportunity to decide who's in control of his life, where his control center is. Are we going to act, or are we going to react? Are we going to let others control us by their mood swings or their sour manners, or are we going to have that sense of inner balance that lets us respond to the world in the way we choose?

"Nobody," says Harris, "is unhappier than the perpetual reactor." He is always at the mercy of other people and other events. He has unwittingly handed his emotional center over to somebody else, and like a yo-yo he goes up and down as somebody else pulls the string. Is he complimented? Then he has that false euphoria that quickly fades because it was not born of self-approval. Is he criticized? Every unkind word cuts to the bone because he has no sense of self —except according to what others say. The reactor moves cautiously through every day with his eyes cast over his shoulder, always wondering what other people think of him. He returns unkindness for unkindness, blow for blow, because his control center is not in himself. It is rooted someplace else. And someplace else is a most dangerous place for such a precious possession.

Would we let a stranger control our wealth or property? Would we let someone we don't know control our child's upbringing? Some perhaps do, but wisdom would dictate we do otherwise. Why, then, let strangers or the colleagues that we meet each day control us? Why would we ever relinquish the control of our most priceless possession, our personalities?

My friend Marion D. Hanks tells the story of a young marine who was uneasy and didn't know why.

"There were plenty of ordinary reasons for a member of a combat unit in almost daily contact with the enemy to feel uneasy, but this was something different. When he returned with his group to their base camp after several days in the field, he discovered what it was.

" 'C'mon, Smith,' the sergeant said. 'The whole outfit's going into town. This time you're coming with us even if we have to drag you. You are about to find out how big men live when they get away from their mamas.'

"Rick Smith caught the sharp edge of the other's voice, knifing through the seeming lightness of his words. He understood the look in the eye and the tightness at the corners of the mouth. Sarge wasn't kidding; he really intended to take Rick along, even if he had to drag him.

" 'No thanks, Sarge,' Rick said. 'I'm staying here.'

" 'Listen, Sonny,' came the grim answer, 'big men can make up their own minds about their lives. They don't stay tied to Mommy's apron strings when they're in this man's outfit. You're coming with us.'

"Rick Smith could feel the color drain from his face and the strength ebb from his knees, but his voice surprised him with its calmness as he heard himself answer:

" 'You're right, Sarge, a big man can make up his own mind. I have the responsibility to decide whether I'll live the way you do or the way I believe in. You've made *your* choice, Sergeant, and that's your business. But I still have a choice, and I prefer to live another way. That's what I've made up my mind to do. I'm staying here.' " (*Now and Forever* [Salt Lake City: Bookcraft, 1974], pp. 5–6.)

He made a wise decision on who controlled his life.

But who's in control in your life? Where's the control center? Is your face a piece of clay to be molded into tears or frowns by every passing person? Do you hang on the approval of others or slink away when you've been shunned? Do you shout in anger at a member of your family and then excuse yourself saying, "She made me do it"? Who's in control in your life, anyway? The answer to that question for you, the answer for each of us, depends on our maturity level.

It's almost painful to watch the contortions of the child or teenager whose emotional center of control is fixed outside himself. In order to gain approval the teenager feels compelled to wear just a certain kind of clothes, laugh at a certain kind of joke. He twists his personality into a certain shape to fit in. The child feels devastated if someone else gets a compliment. "Don't you love me, too, Daddy?" he says. Or he gets into a fight with another child and when asked why he hit her, he says, "She did it first." Meaning, of course, that he had to; he had no other choice.

But as we grow up we hope to leave these vestiges of childhood behind. For the sake of serenity, we hope that we can become the masters of our own attitudes and actions. How fickle our emotions would be if we were depressed or elated all in response to someone else's whim! How like a weathercock in the wind we must be if we find this phrase always rushing to our lips—"You made me do it." Nobody makes us do anything. Our responses to the world start in our spirit and in our brain. We send the messages down the network of nerves to our face and our tongue; we control what we are and what we do. That privilege or burden belongs to nobody else.

Let me conclude this chapter by giving you three ideas to help you gain that sense of inner balance that will put you in control of yourself.

First, set self-possession as a goal. Make the conscious decision that you want to act and not react toward your world.

Second, learn to value yourself enough so that you do not need to look to someone else to find out who you are. Someone else's gloom or cheer toward you may have nothing to do with you at all. You certainly don't need to respond in kind.

Third, draw close enough to the Lord that His loving estimation of you can be your ballast for the changing winds of fortune or popularity in your life.

Ultimately, your prize possession will be your ability to control yourself. It was Cicero, the great Roman orator, who said very simply and profoundly: "Control thyself." It is one thing to know who you are but another to control the capacity that you have. Your most prized possession will always be self-possession.

Chapter 8

"By Faith All Things Are Fulfilled"

Dr. Jo Ann Larsen, a family therapist, gave some wise and practical counsel on teaching children and building their self-esteem. She reminded us of the tendency most parents have, in their efforts to teach their children responsibility, of so often stressing the negative things the children do —the mistakes and misjudgments they make, the inconveniences and trouble they cause. She made the statement that between birth and twenty years of age the average child gets from parents, teachers, siblings, and peers probably one hundred thousand negative messages, which are rarely balanced by positive messages. With an extremely lucky child, the ratio would probably be ten negatives to one positive, which she claims can, in itself, be highly damaging, often for life, to a child's feelings of self-worth.

She encourages us all to develop lenses through which we can see positives instead of negatives, thus making it possible to perform miracles sometimes and certainly to greatly improve the results of our teaching efforts and parent-child relationships. (From the manuscript of Jo Ann Larsen's forthcoming book *I'm a Day Late and a Dollar Short, and It's OK: A Woman's Survival Guide for the '90s,* due for publication in 1991 by Deseret Book Co.)

The good accomplished toward the making of a better world through upbuilding, trusting approaches to life situations, in contrast to those that tear down, could very possibly never be accurately assessed.

Why is it that as humans we tend to emphasize the negative when there is so much to be positive about? We constantly criticize our children and each other, find fault, are judgmental, and so often seem to seek out and build up people's weaknesses and failings rather than their strengths and successes.

Also, in our own personal life-styles there are those of us who are incessant, chronic worriers. We worry about all the negative things that could happen, but which usually don't, rather than positively trying to face problems with some amount of faith and hope of success. Then, in our society, for some reason, we seem to dwell on the bizarre, the tragic, the profane, and the evils of our day. So often the newspaper and television reports center attention on the negative aspects of life: teenage suicides, drugs, AIDS, murders, infidelities, dishonesty, and a host of other social ills.

As I have traveled throughout the Church, I occasionally see another form of thinking that can become quite negative—members weighted down, sometimes grimly, with the serious tasks they must perform to earn livings, pay mortgages, rear children, faithfully fulfill Church callings, attend to school and community responsibilities, live righteously and worthily—the list could go on and on.

I often think that for some of these people the joy and excitement have gone out of their lives and that all they look back on are crowded, grim days, often filled with great guilt because of the pressure of trying to accomplish everything they think is necessary and to be perfect right now. Interestingly, negative attitudes seem to affect us in this way.

Now, of course, life is serious. Children must be taught, bills must be paid, we must live righteously —it is the Lord's counsel to us. We can't help but worry sometimes, as there are and always will be never-ending negatives existing all around us which must be faced, dealt with, and solved. But I wonder if the constant bombardment of personal and nationwide dilemmas, challenges, and seemingly hopeless situations don't sometimes frustrate and depress us to the point where our minds are distracted from the very principles that would allow us to rise above the negative and find the positive answers we need.

In spite of the many negative occurrences in life, there are those who seem to have the knack of seeing the positive side of most things. A young businessman was opening a new branch office, and a friend sent a floral arrangement to help celebrate the occasion. When the friend arrived at the opening he was appalled to find that the wreath bore the inscription "Rest in Peace." Angry, he later complained to the florist. After apologizing, the florist said, "Look at it this way. Somewhere today a man was buried under a wreath that said, 'Good luck in your new location.' "

In the Book of Mormon, a book in which we find so many answers and so much direction in solving problems, there is a scripture that, to me, sheds great light on this matter of a positive, trusting, hopeful attitude of faith as a substitute for facing life's problems with discouragement and despair. Listen to the words of the prophet Ether as he exhorts us to know and believe in God as a foundation of hope and faith.

"By faith all things are fulfilled—wherefore, whoso believeth in God might with surety hope for a better world, yea, even a place at the right hand of God, which hope cometh of faith, maketh an anchor to the souls of men, which would make them sure and steadfast, always abounding in good works, being led to glorify God" (Ether 12:3–4).

Throughout the whole of this marvelous chapter of Ether, we are taught the wonders accomplished by faith, love, and hope. It seems to me that dwelling on negative thoughts and approaches is, in fact, working directly opposite of the principle of faith—in the Lord, ourselves, and others—and causes continual feelings of gloom, while the positive lifts and buoys us up, encourages us to forge ahead, and is an attitude that can be developed, a habit that can be cultivated.

The epitome of celebrating the beautiful and overlooking misfortune is this story of Thomas Moore.

Soon after he was married, Thomas Moore, the famous nineteenth-century Irish poet, was called away on a business trip. Upon his return he was met at the door, not by his beautiful bride, but by the family doctor.

"Your wife is upstairs," said the doctor. "But she asked that you not come up." And then Moore learned the terrible truth: his wife had contracted smallpox. The disease had left her once flawless skin pocked and scarred. She had taken one look at her reflection in the mirror and commanded that the shutters be drawn and that her husband never see her again. Moore would not listen. He ran upstairs and threw open the door of his wife's room. It was black as night inside. Not a sound came from the darkness. Groping along the wall, Moore felt for the gas jets.

A startled cry came from a black corner of the room. "No! Don't light the lamps!"

Moore hesitated, swayed by the pleading in the voice.

"Go!" she begged. "Please go! This is the greatest gift I can give you now."

Moore did go. He went down to his study, where he sat up most of the night, prayerfully writing. Not a poem this time, but a song. He had never written a song before, but now he found it more natural to his mood than simple poetry. He not only wrote the words, but he wrote the music too. And the next morning, as soon as the sun was up he returned to his wife's room.

He felt his way to a chair and sat down. "Are you awake?" he asked.

"I am," came a voice from the far side of the room. "But you must not ask to see me. You must not press me, Thomas."

"I will sing to you, then," he answered. And so for the first time, Thomas Moore sang to his wife the song that still lives today:

"Believe me, if all those endearing young charms which I gaze on so fondly today, were to change by tomorrow and flee in my arms like fairy gifts fading away, thou wouldst still be adored, as this moment thou art—let thy loveliness fade as it will."

Moore heard a movement from the dark corner where his wife lay in her loneliness, waiting. He continued:

"Let thy loveliness fade as it will, and around the dear ruin each wish of my heart would entwine itself verdantly still—"

The song ended. As his voice trailed off on the last note, Moore heard his bride rise. She crossed the room to the window, reached up, and slowly drew open the shutters.

We need more such attitudes in the world. There is the story of the husband and wife who had saved and saved for a new car. After taking delivery, the husband told his wife that all of the necessary legal documents and insurance information were in a packet in the glove compartment. On her first day out in the new car, she was involved in an accident which demolished the car's front end. Unhurt, in tears, and near panic she opened the packet to show the police officer her papers. There she found a handwritten note from her husband which read: "Now that you have had an accident, remember I can always replace the car, but not you. Please know how much I love you!"

As stated in the beginning that with children we so often see the negative before the positive, a little boy was almost squelched in his attempt to express his feelings because an adult didn't understand. A special friend of mine, Dr. Thomas Myers, shared this tender experience:

A small boy accompanied his grandparents into Dr. Myers's medical office. The old man was leaning on the boy's two upstretched hands as he moved. The child encouraged him with, "Come on, Grandpa, you can make it! . . . Only a little farther, Grandpa. . . . The doctor will make your leg better." A sweet grandmother walked behind.

After the visit, the three exited the same way. The little boy was given a helium balloon on his way out.

He helped his grandfather to the car, then ran back in and, pulling himself up to the counter, asked the receptionist, "Please, may I have another balloon?"

His grandmother, still standing there, scolded him, "Of course you can't. I warned you not to let that balloon go!" She apologized to the receptionist. "He did this last week—went right outside and let his balloon go. I really did warn him this time."

The little boy was trying to tell her something. She bent down to listen. Then, with tears showing on her thin, wrinkled face, the grandmother asked, "Could he please have another balloon? You see, his little sister died a few months ago, and he wanted her to have a balloon to play with too!"

As critical and judgmental as we often must be, as much as we will have to correct, as truly as we must face unpleasant realities all our days, let us recognize and praise the thousands of beauties of life around us; the many wonderful examples of virtuous living; the strengths and courage of so many souls; the exceptional talents and achievements of our family members, neighbors, and associates; the countless blessings that we have been given. As has been quoted so many times but fits here so well,

Two men looked out through the selfsame bars:
One saw the mud, the other saw the stars.

And as Mormon has taught:
"But charity [in this case, the charity in our thinking and appreciation of others] is the pure love of Christ, and it endureth forever; and whoso is found possessed of it at the last day, it shall be well with him" (Moroni 7:47).

PART II

Being

Chapter 9

''As a Man Thinketh''

Every big city has its special street. In Los Angeles, it's Hollywood or Sunset boulevards; in San Francisco, it's Broadway; in New York, it's Times Square. And what do these streets have most regrettably in common? There under harsh neon lights, in dark corners, beneath lurid signs, a plague of pornography assaults the souls of men.

Have you seen the signs—those signs of the times? ''Adults only,'' they read. ''See it all,'' they invite. And there with sleazy photos, cheap films, and glossy men's and women's magazines, the profiteers of porn are making over five billion dollars a year by filling our minds and hearts with filth. *Time* magazine has labeled this the age of porn, and very well it may be—if you and I don't do something about it.

Do you know that some 780 American theaters, including many formerly elegant family houses, now routinely show X-rated movies fifty-two weeks a year? Do you know that even small communities in America's conservative heartland now have bars featuring suggestive dancers and bizarre conduct? Do you know that in 1989 alone over three thousand complaints were reported to the Federal Communications Commission for obscenities and street language in rock music played on the air—songs your teenagers probably heard on their favorite radio station?

What we face as a society reminds me of the story about a boy who received a calf for his birthday. Each morning the boy dutifully carried his calf up the mountain to the grassy pastures to feed. This was fine for a time, but every day as that calf would feed, it would gain a pound or two and, of course, very gradually the calf grew into a cow. At first the boy didn't notice the extra weight, but day after day as that calf put on pounds, the weight became more difficult to bear. Finally when the calf became a hefty one thousand pounds, the boy collapsed while he tried to climb the mountain, and that's where we'll leave this sad story.

Can you see the parallel? What we labeled as "pornography" twenty years ago is probably fit for prime-time television this year. What shocked us a decade ago is probably run-of-the-mill to our sensibilities today. Ronald Butt wrote the following in the London *Times*: "The history of the Roman arena instructs us how the appetite of a people can be created by what is fed to it—the upper classes of Rome were systematically addicted by their rulers to the frenzy and titillation of sadistic violence by a steady progression from less to more until the Roman character itself was conditioned to a coarse insensibility to suffering" (as quoted in Neal A. Maxwell, *Deposition of a Disciple* [Salt Lake City: Deseret Book Co., 1976], p. 17).

We have marvelled from our twentieth-century, civilized perspective that the Romans could have laughed and revelled while they watched men—human beings, living souls—fight to the death in the gladiators' arena. But that insensitivity to suffering didn't happen all at once. At first, perhaps just a little violence titillated their emotions. But then a little violence grew boring. It took more and more, that steady progression from less to more, to bring them to the shocking point where they could watch fights to the death for casual pleasure.

We are seeing today that same trend with pornography. Gradually our society is accepting practices long considered immoral. And the upshot for all of us is that our sensitivities are brutalized and coarsened. Our standards are subverted, our appetites vulgarized.

There are some who say pornography is just the natural outgrowth of our newer, permissive society. I wonder if slipping national test scores, increased crime, and juvenile delinquency are also a natural outgrowth of this permissiveness. If so, I ask, when are we going to reassert old standards—standards that involve self-control, self-restraint, and self-mastery? When will we realize that the old phrase ''anything goes'' ultimately means that everything goes—everything lovely, praiseworthy, and uplifting about life gets trampled in the chase for mere sensationalism.

The thought, ''As a man thinketh, so is he,'' is the greatest truth in character formation. As James Allen said: ''A man is literally *what he thinks*, his character being the complete sum of all his thoughts.

''As the plant springs from, and could not be without, the seed, so every act of a man springs from the hidden seeds of thought, and could not have appeared without them. This applies equally to those acts called 'spontaneous' and 'unpremeditated' as to those which are deliberately executed." (*As A Man Thinketh* [Salt Lake City: Bookcraft, n.d.], p. 11.)

When I notice the flood of pornography deluging our senses, I remember with Allen that "man is made or unmade by himself; in the armory of thought he forges the weapons by which he destroys himself; he also fashions the tools with which he builds for himself heavenly mansions of joy and strength and peace. By the right choice and true application of thought, man ascends to the Divine Perfection; by the abuse and wrong application of thought, he descends below the level of the beast. Between these two extremes are all the grades of character, and man is their maker and master." (*As A Man Thinketh*, p. 13.)

"As a man thinketh, so is he." Martin Luther tells us that "the prosperity of a country depends not on the abundance of its revenues, not on the strength of its fortifications, nor on the beauty of its public buildings, but consists of the number of its people of enlightenment and character." There's a sermon in a sentence!

For those who think there's nothing so adult about adult bookstores, who believe there's nothing particularly mature about programs for mature audiences only, listen to the words of a modern prophet. He said: "As citizens, join in the fight against obscenity in your communities. Do not be lulled into inaction by the pornographic profiteers who say that to remove obscenity is to deny people the rights of free chioce. Do not let them masquerade licentiousness as liberty." (Spencer W. Kimball, *The Teachings of Spencer W. Kimball*, ed. Edward L. Kimball [Salt Lake City: Bookcraft, 1982], p. 285.)

We can all do something about pornography. Do you believe it? I know of one metropolitan city whose citizens organized themselves and picketed X-rated movie theaters with the result that half of those theaters in the city closed their doors. In San Pedro, California, civic and religious leaders banded together to close a movie theater that specialized in adult entertainment and that was located just a block and a half from the elementary school. It took them sixty-nine days of picketing, but the theater did go out of business. It seems patrons were ashamed to be seen by those picketing, and business came to a halt.

And on a personal level, you can do something about the evil influence flooding your senses. All it takes is a little courage. Courage to walk away from the dirty joke. Courage to turn off the knob on your television or radio when a program doesn't meet your standards. Courage to avoid the unseemly movie, even if it's the talk of the town, and courage to get up and walk out of a theater even though some might think of us as "too good."

Have you ever seen a piece of desert glass? That's what they call old bottles that have been left for years in the desert in the sand and the sun. After those years the bottles are no longer clear. Instead they take on a blue or purple tint and they are *permanently stained*. Our minds are a little like desert glass. They can become permanently colored, stained by what we let pass through them.

Let's join the fight against evil, if not on a public level, at least on a private one. As Charles C. Colton said: "The only things in which we can be said to have any ownership are our actions. Our thoughts may be bad, yet produce no poison; they may be good, yet produce no fruit. Our riches may be taken from us by misfortune, our reputation by malice, our spirits by calamity, our health by disease, our friends by death, but our actions must follow us beyond the grave.''

Now is the time to assert our basic values in all places and let our personal behavior back up what we say. Courage will be our best armor. Consider the following account of such courage as related by Neal A. Maxwell: ''Outnumbered by the Persians, according to legend, the Spartans had to hold the pass at Thermopylae. After failing to take the pass, the Persians sent an emissary to the Spartans, who asked them to surrender and threatened them by saying that the Persians had so many archers they could 'darken the sky with their arrows.' The Spartans replied: 'So much the better, we shall fight in the shade.' '' (''*For the Power Is in Them . . .*'' [Salt Lake City: Deseret Book Co., 1970], p. 51.)

Chapter 10

"School Thy Feelings"

One autumn, a giant jet airliner crashed into Boston Harbor. Sixty-two people were killed and tons of wreckage were strewn across the fields. Upon investigation, the cause of the terrible accident was discovered. Starlings, tiny birds, had been sucked into the air scoops and had choked the massive engines. Nothing but a flight of little birds. What a trifle to bring down so much! But how typical of life, for isn't it the trifles, the mere nothings, that choke the soaring of our own souls?

How often we think, "I could be so great, I could be so fine, if it weren't for the constant irritations and conflicts in my life." It is the little bits of things that fret and annoy us. It is the pinpricks that often make us explode into anger. We let inconsequentials contaminate our happy days.

Think about what last made you angry; what was it that made ugly words escape your mouth? What made your pulse quicken or your collar hot? Was it just because a driver cut in front of you and stole your lane? (I think the term "national temper" must refer to all of us at commuting hour.) Was it just because your child acted childish and cried for what he wanted?

I remember hearing about a young Frenchman who was pushing his son's baby carriage down the street. The youngster was howling with rage. "Please, Bernard, control yourself," the father said quietly. "Easy there, Bernard, keep calm!"

"Congratulations, monsieur," said a woman who had been watching. "You know just how to speak to infants—calmly and gently." Then she said, "So the little fellow's named Bernard?"

"No, madame," corrected the father. "He's named Andre. I'm Bernard."

A well-adjusted parent is one who can enjoy the scenery even with the kids in the backseat.

Did you last get angry just because you were running a few minutes late? People who are quick to take offense will never run short of supply.

Someone has said that the measure of a man is the things that make him angry. And I believe that we have plenty of confirmation of this statement in the life and teachings of Jesus, as well as in the experiences of other noble souls who have lived since His time.

We note that, although Jesus warned His disciples against the evil results of uncontrolled temper, He became angry himself, and on at least one occasion He was prepared to use force, if necessary, in driving evil practices from the halls of the temple.

But think, if you will, of the size of the things that aroused His anger. Men called Him the prince of devils, and He paid little attention to their criticism. They had said that He was blasphemous, but this had not caused Him to lose His temper. They had spit in His face, mocked Him, hit Him, and later even nailed Him to the cross, ripping His flesh and causing excruciating pain, but He did not lose control of His feelings. What marvelous self-conquest!

It was quite different, however, when they criticized Him for doing good on the Sabbath. Realizing that the Sabbath was made for man, and not man for the Sabbath, He started to heal a poor fellow on the sacred day. And when He found the crowd in a critical mood, He "looked round about on them with anger" (Mark 3:5).

So long as men held Him up personally to ridicule, He paid little attention. But in the presence of injustice, when men would be unfair and unkind toward each other, He threw the influence of His great tempered personality against their evil practices. No one could hurt Him by attempting to punish Him as an individual, but they touched His heart when they were cruel to each other.

Let us not confuse the well-controlled use of unselfish enthusiasm with the harsh roaring of a weak, tempestuous spirit. In the teachings of Jesus there is a definite place for the former; there is neither time nor place for the latter. "Ye have heard that it was said by them of old time, Thou shalt not kill; and whosoever shall kill shall be in danger of the judgment: but I say unto you, That whosoever is angry with his brother . . . shall be in danger of the judgment" (Matthew 5:21–22).

One comic said it this way, "Say what you think when you're angry and you'll make the best speech you'll ever live to regret."

Think of the words to this song penned by Charles W. Penrose:

School thy feelings, O my brother;
Train thy warm, impulsive soul.
Do not its emotions smother,
But let wisdom's voice control.
School thy feelings; there is power
In the cool, collected mind.
Passion shatters reason's tower,
Makes the clearest vision blind.
("School Thy Feelings," *Hymns,* no. 336.)

What's the size of the thing that makes you angry? What little things can splinter your inner harmony?

One New Year's Eve a friend of mine made a very interesting new year's resolution. He swore on that occasion that he would not commit another sin as long as he lived. He said he had made a lot of mistakes in the past, but from now on he was going to exercise perfect self-control. When another friend started to make fun of him and his resolution, the first man became so angry that he put up his fists.

Contrast that with the temper of famous scientist George Washington Carver. When he was told that he had lost his life's savings, seventy thousand dollars, in the crash of an Alabama bank, Dr. Carver said mildly, "I guess somebody found a use for it. I was not using it myself."

Why let your days be ruined by trifles? We have to have a plan for those times when we feel the hot emotions begin to bubble over like burning lava.

One young mother told me that when her three preschoolers begin to pique her spirits, when she longs to shout or scream or cry, she escapes to the bathroom, locks the door, and says a prayer for help. "Let me stay calm," she prays. "Bless me with patience and love. Let thy serenity settle upon me in this angry hour."

I have found the same thing works for me. When I was newly married I felt ill and a little blue one day at work, so I left my office a little early to go home. The heavy traffic of the Los Angeles freeway did nothing but add to my anxieties. When I arrived home, I found that my wife was not there. Here I was expecting tender love, care, and understanding, and of all days she could have picked, this was the one she decided not to be at home. I couldn't imagine why she couldn't read my mind.

At home I grew more angry with each moment that she was absent. And then finally, after I had spent about an hour of anxious waiting, she appeared on the scene. I looked at her somewhat wonderingly and asked where she had been. Can you imagine what she had been doing? Shopping!

"Couldn't you have been more thoughtful of your husband?" I said.

She responded, "I couldn't have known that you were coming home early."

I was still a bit upset.

She wanted to show me the treasures she had just purchased, and I wasn't particularly interested. One by one she unwrapped the various items, and finally getting to the one she had saved for the big surprise, she said, "Just wait until you see the material that I finally found to cover the couch." And she showed it to me. She said, "What do you think?"

I said, "It is terrible."

She was hurt, and with her emotions showing, she left the room. An hour passed. And you know, women sometimes have an interesting way of striking back. Without saying a word, she just did not fix supper.

Well, one act begets another, and I thought, "Two can play this game." So I resorted to that "adult" game called the silent treatment. I didn't talk to her for the rest of the evening, and she responded by not even answering.

Hours later when we had had time to ponder, a whole new feeling came over us. We had schooled our feelings. Remember it's not your position that can make you happy; it's your disposition.

In your moments of anger, when starlings would choke your engines, seek your Heavenly Father. Since he has given us the commandment to avoid anger, he is anxious to help us keep it. And is it worth the effort? Let a trifle rob you of your serenity today, and you may find the happiness of all your days is stolen forever in little discontents.

Chapter 11

"Blessed Are the Peacemakers"

It's the easiest thing in the world to find something to disagree about, especially with those in your own family. There you are, a jumble of different personalities with different needs and different tastes and different maturity levels, all trying to be one in loyalty and love, all sharing the same TV, the same dinner table, the same four walls. Sometimes it's hard to avoid conflict.

I recall a story about the little boy who had misbehaved and was going to be spanked for it. When his dad asked him if he had anything to say, the youngster asked, "Did Grandpa spank you when you were little?"

The father nodded. "Yes, he did."

"And did Grandpa's father spank him?" the boy asked.

"That's right," replied the father.

"And did Great Grandpa's father spank him?" the boy pursued.

"Yes," said the father, weakening a little, "I suppose he did."

"Well, then," said the youngster, "don't you think it's about time we stopped this inherited brutality?"

Parents and children, husbands and wives, want desperately to get along together in these, our most important relationships. But unfortunately, it is often on those within our own home, the people closest to us, that we take out our anxieties, our pressures, and our tensions. We may smile very sweetly for the crowd we'll never see again, but get us home, and we let it roar.

I heard one wife say that her husband was taking the instability of the economy lately with great difficulty. In fact, she said that she thought they were going to remake the movie *Old Yeller*. This time it wouldn't be about a dog; it would be about her husband as he tried to pay their monthly bills.

Well, there are ways to handle our high anxieties. There are tools we can each employ to bring harmony into our homes. If you want to be a peacemaker at home, listen to these ten steps. They are worth your time and effort now for the future of you and your family.

1. Accept the fact of difference. No two human beings are alike. Social scientists have described about 127 ways in which husbands and wives can possibly differ. Think, for example, of a simple thing like temperature preference. He's a fresh-air fiend. He likes it cold, sleeping with the window open in the middle of January. She, on the other hand, likes it warm. She can't stand to be cold. She wouldn't roll

down the window in the middle of July if she had her choice. And here they are, married. What is she to do? Shiver her way through life? Or is he to sweat? Maybe they'll just fight about it forever and ever.

It certainly is rare that husbands and wives are alike in all 127 areas of compatibility. She's affectionate; he is formal. She is an organizer who likes everything in its place; he throws his shoes and socks on the floor. She likes movies; he likes sports. But for the sake of a marriage we must accept each other as we are. We cannot remake our spouse in our own image; we cannot assume there is something wrong with our partner because he or she is not exactly like us. Without screaming, without fighting, we have to learn to compromise, accepting the differences between us.

The same is true with parents and children. Children are not always just who you want them to be. They do not always respond in the same way to your discipline. I heard one mother of eight say that she had to approach the disciplining of each child in her family differently. One child responded to her new methods of handling problems, while another rebelled at the same. And so it goes. Everyone is different, even in our own families. To get along peacefully, we have to accept those differences and accommodate them.

2. For increased harmony in your home, face each problem as it arises. Ask yourself, "What is the trouble here?" Try to sense how you really feel about it, and discuss it calmly with each other. There is nothing worse than family members who store up grievances against one another until they boil over in resentment and bitterness. Can you imagine the rancor that is felt by both parties when one is giving to the other this kind of speech: "Well, last Saturday

you did this, and last June you did that, and Christmas of 1978 you did this." Trust and love are destroyed as one is attacked with stored up anger. Instead, face each problem as it arises.

3. When there is anger arising in the home, look for the causes of the conflict. Ask yourself, "What are we really fighting about? Is it worth the rupture in our relationship." For example, when a husband and wife fight for a half an hour about something as trivial as whether or not he has taken care of a chore, both need to step back and ask themselves what the problem is really about. Is one or the other just looking for a scapegoat on whom to take out some feelings of pressure or misery? Is there a deeper reason than the obvious? Maybe she is angry, not just about the chore, but also about the fact that he doesn't help her enough around the house or doesn't appreciate her efforts there.

At any rate, when you find yourself responding in anger to a family member, ask yourself, "What are the causes of the conflict here?"

4. The next step to family harmony is to put your goals and values into words. Ask yourself, "What am I after in this struggle? What does it matter to me? Why am I so upset about it?" Define for yourself not just the causes of the conflict, but also what you really want to achieve by it. You may find that in a struggle a calm discussion of your goals will clarify for you and the other person what really is the matter, while arguing about it may only confuse the issue.

5. Consider the outcome of this problem, "Where are we really headed in this struggle?" What is the question here? Take again the husband who likes to sleep in the cold and his wife who likes it warm. Is it always going to be a personal struggle between them, with his kicking off the covers and her pulling them

back on? Or can one or the other of them do some adapting? To what extent can they learn to live happily with the difference that bothers them now? When you are in a conflict with a family member, consider the outcome of the problem and be willing to adapt yourself.

6. Rather than constantly defending your territory, stop long enough to see how it feels to be the other person. There are at least two sides to every conflict. Can you put down your cannon long enough to listen to what the other person is really saying? Can you pull out of yourself and empathize for a minute? The preschooler who stubbornly refuses to pick up her bedroom may simply be overwhelmed by the task of organization. The husband who didn't take out that garbage may simply not have understood that his wife expected that of him. How does the other person engaged in a momentary battle with you really feel and why?

7. Consider your alternatives. After you've defined the problem, brainstorm for solutions that will be mutually acceptable to both of you. The husband and wife who had different temperature preferences finally got an electric blanket with dual control. There are all kinds of ways to solve a problem. And when children are fighting in the home, you might calmly sit down with them and try the "we" approach. What are "we" going to do to solve this situation? Ask them to come up with some unique solutions to their problem that will make everybody winners in the struggle. Children often have better ideas than we think they do—better, sometimes, than those we have. The ones who have a part in making the rules are the best supporters.

8. After you've thought of your solutions, make a plan of action and follow it through. Determine to-

gether who will do what and how in the proposed plan of action. Make sure that each person gets a real chance to suggest what he will do to help rather than be told what to do by some dominant member of the family.

9. Get to know yourself and each other as you solve your problems. Determine how your particular personality faces confrontation. Is it with anger? Defensiveness? Withdrawal? Pray that you may come to a deeper understanding of yourself so that you can handle conflict better and better.

10. And finally, make sure that your family has something beyond its own personal needs to live for. We must all have a purpose in life that extends beyond ourselves. A family that kneels together in sincere prayer cannot long remain angry at each other. Parents who wish to train up their children in the way they should go must go in the way they would have their children go (see Proverbs 22:6).

So, if you are in a season of snarling at your house, step back and resolve to be a peacemaker. Accept your differences, search for solutions together, tune up your ears instead of your vocal cords. There aren't any hopeless situations—only people who have come to feel hopeless about them. It was Voltaire who said: ''Perfection is attained by slow degrees; she requires the hand of time.''

Chapter 12

Next Time

Recently it was my privilege to address several thousand youth in a seminar on helping America become drug free. As a part of my presentation I quoted some interesting statistics published by Abigail Van Buren (Dear Abby) in one of her columns and some from a local news source. The information listed below is part of what occurred in a typical day in the United States at the time the data was gathered. Note:

— 9,077 babies were born (1,282 illegitimate).
— 2,750 kids ran away from home.
— 63,288 automobile accidents occurred in which 129 people died.
— 5,962 couples were wed; 1,986 divorced.

— 56,000 animals were turned over to animal shelters, and 36,986 dogs and cats were put to death there.
— 1,370 men underwent vasectomies.
— A woman was raped every eight minutes; someone was murdered every 27 minutes and someone robbed every 78 seconds; a burglar struck every 10 seconds; and a car was stolen every 33 seconds.
— 2,466 children were bitten by dogs.
— $54,794 was spent to fight dandruff.
— Camera bugs took 19,178,000 snapshots.
— 679 million telephone conversations occurred, of which 50 million were long-distance calls.
— 3 bike riders were killed in accidents; 15 people drowned.
— Tobacco chewers chewed 1.3 million packages of plug tobacco.
— People drank 90 million cans of beer.
— 2,750 persons were arrested on drunk charges.
— 2,740 teenagers got pregnant (over 1,000 under the influence of a chemical).
— 3,321 women had abortions.
— 5,200 people died (of these, 1,070 died of cancer due to smoking).
— Over 2,000 babies were born addicted to drugs.
— 187 people died from a drug overdose.
— 37 teenagers committed suicide from drug-related depression.
— Thousands of our youth will begin some kind of drug dependency today.

Such a report could be most discouraging, and of course it is a matter of great concern. Fortunately, however, the majority of youth in our society do not get involved in such harmful activity. Hopefully the many who don't participate in these things can and will, in some way, be of help in bringing about an influence for good on those in our communities who are in trouble in so many ways, as indicated by the aforementioned list. As Lois Wyse observed:

In a world where
Bad deeds are celebrated
And good ones relegated
To page 49 of the paper,
Where first place goes to push and
shove
And the cost of things is put above
The cost of time together,
Isn't it wonderful that,
From time to time,
The best of us
Reach out and touch
The rest of us?

(Reprinted with permission from the September 1985 *Reader's Digest*, p. 187.)

Note in an excerpt from a letter I received recently the desire of one wonderful but very experienced person to do just that (used by permission):

"I am a prescription drug addict and almost without exception every transgression that I committed was related to my drug use.

"No less than five different times I overdosed, and ended up in the hospital in the intensive care unit.

"I really had no choice at this point. I was and am an addict as much as the cocaine or heroin addict off the street.

"I am alive today only through the grace of God, although as my addiction and disease progressed, I gave up on God and gave Him only lip service. He never gave up on me. There was a point in time when the drugs I was using became my best friend, my family, my lover, and even my God. There was absolutely nothing as important as getting and using drugs. My life was one continual lie. I not only lied all the time, I also cheated, stole, misused people, abused trusts, abused friendships, and even abused the Church. I stole from my employers, my wife, my children, my parents, my brother and sister, my wife's family, and many, many friends. I put the careers of doctors, dentists, and pharmacists in jeopardy through my lying and manipulating. I basically went against every moral, ethical, and spiritual value that had meant the most to me. If only I had listened to those who warned me.

"I am very ashamed of all that I have done and write to you in this way only to try to illustrate to you what it is or can be that people can be up against. And there are more and more people every day that are caught in this circumstance. If only I hadn't depended on those pills.

"I only wish to reach out to people and warn them before it is too late, and also to let others who are already abusing prescription drugs know that there is help and hope.

"I don't know if you are aware of just how bad this problem is, or if you really know that much about it, but I have really only scratched the surface with this letter.

"Please help me to help others before they, too, have such stories to tell—if only they are still alive."

This person's experience illustrates all too clearly how pronounced the drug problem can be. And we all greatly need to understand the reality of that fact.

Often we tend to think that those who are addicts are on heroin, cocaine, alcohol, tobacco, and related drugs, but there is wide misuse of prescription drugs by individuals and in families whom we consider very normal. Such was the case in the life of the person who wrote the above letter.

Fortunately the medical world today has seen and taken action against the terrible destruction drugs are having on the population of the world. In the United States great strides are being made to reduce or eliminate the use of tobacco and other forms of dependence. The various campaigns expounded today have caused me to reflect on certain times in my past when I observed firsthand some of these challenges.

I remember when I was a private in the army, I bunked next to a young fellow who was a compulsive smoker. I watched him for some time before I finally got the nerve to ask him this: "Say, how does it feel to be a prisoner?"

"You're in the army, too," he said.

"No, I don't mean that," I said. "How does it feel to be chained up to a habit like smoking? I've been watching you for some time and I think you're a slave to your cigarettes."

"I am not," he answered. "I could go without these anytime I wanted to."

Well, who could resist the challenge at a moment like that? I told him that if that were true, he wouldn't mind proving it to me by going one more hour without smoking. That shouldn't be so hard for somebody like him who could go without cigarettes anytime he wanted to.

He agreed. He was eager, he said, to prove to me that he was not a slave to the cigarette habit. We set up my watch to time the hour; he handed me his cigarettes and the challenge was on.

The first two minutes, he did well. He looked like

a champion. No habit was going to make a fool out of him! But as the time wore on, he began to get jittery. He didn't know what to do with his hands, twisting them together, sometimes drumming his fingers against the bed.

Finally at the end of forty minutes, he admitted that he couldn't stand it any longer. He didn't want to prove anything to anybody; he just wanted a cigarette.

Most of us, like my army friend, are positive that we are in control of our habits. We see ourselves as the masters of our souls, the captains of our ships. "We'd never get in a wreck," said one couple as they hopped in their car without fastening their seat belts —only to have their car demolished by a drunk driver that very night. "That wouldn't happen to me. I know what I'm doing. I'm in control." These are the sentiments that most of us feel when we hear health or safety warnings.

Here's one, for example: "Warning: Smoking is dangerous to your health." Words to that effect appear on every package of cigarettes and in every cigarette ad. But how many smokers think it applies to them? Many of them probably see it as a far distant threat, like a tiny storm cloud on the horizon.

And how do you think that warning about the dangers of smoking affects the very young who take up the habit? Undoubtedly you know what it is like to be so young and think good health and good fortune will always be yours. It's an optimistic time, when things like lung cancer and heart disease have no meaning at all. So in many of the elementary schools across our country, youngsters sneak off to the rest rooms to smoke, and in research studies back in 1976 it was estimated that over 20,000 teenage girls began that smoking habit each week. During the 1970s, "in a . . . six-year period, smoking by girls between the ages of 12 and 18 nearly doubled." Undoubtedly the figures on teenage boys were as bad. (See Sydney S. Field, "What Smoking Does to Women," *Reader's Digest*, January 1976, p. 95.)

How do we make the warning that smoking is dangerous to your health really stick? For those who smoke, how do we come to believe that it means our lungs, our life, our health? How do we teach our young people that smoking is not alluring or sophisticated, but merely a slow way to poison their bodies?

What if cigarette ads said, "Warning: Smoking wrinkles up your skin and makes you look old before your time"? That information may not be a likely addition to a cigarette ad, but researchers have found that smoking does visible damage to the youthfulness of skin. The basic element for all living cells is oxygen, and when needed oxygen in the blood is displaced by the carbon monoxide of inhaled smoke, there is damage to "every tissue cell in the body—including those of the face." (See Field, "Smoking," p. 97.)

Dr. Harry Daniell, a California internist, did a study on the visible damage of smoking by clinically examining and randomly photographing all the persons between the ages of thirty and seventy who entered his office for a year. "The results were decisive," wrote Sydney S. Field. "In each age group, the most heavily wrinkled class was composed entirely of smokers. . . . Said a report on Daniell's research in Annals of Internal Medicine: 'The association between cigarette smoking and wrinkling was striking in both sexes soon after the age of 30. It was related to the duration and intensity of smoking.

Smokers in the 40-to-49-year age group were likely to be as prominently wrinkled as non-smokers 20 years older.' " ("Smoking," p. 97.)

Or what would you think if you saw a cigarette ad that said, "Warning: Pregnant women who smoke may find that this habit has severely damaged the child they carry"? The U.S. Public Health Service has cited twelve studies in which there has been a significant correlation between cigarette smoking and an elevated infant mortality rate. It has been learned that heavy smoking can produce blood concentrations of carbon monoxide so high that oxygen going to the baby can be reduced as much as 30 percent, robbing the baby of the vitally needed element for growth and life.

In addition, a number of substances causing cancer have been identified in cigarette smoke. These poisons inhaled by the mother can enter the bloodstream of the unborn baby, possibly causing cancer in the child after it is born.

And the powerful drug nicotine, present in all inhaled cigarette smoke, is transmitted directly to the unborn baby, researchers now believe. When nicotine hits the body it has an effect like a sudden fear. Heartbeat escalates, blood pressure rises, and blood vessels contract. What a burden for a developing baby! (See Field, "Smoking," pp. 95–96.)

The warnings against smoking abound. The American Cancer Society did a study of 73,950 men over the age of forty: 36,975 of these were one-pack-a-day smokers, and 36,975 were nonsmokers. In most other respects the men were similar. At the end of the thirty-four-month study, 1,285 smokers had died, while only 662 nonsmokers had died—less than half. The figure showed, surprisingly, that the death rate was higher for all age groups and for all causes among smokers, even among persons dying in accidents or committing suicide. (Information given in the Earl Nightingale program, "Our Changing World," #1056, "If You Can't Quit—Cut Down.")

Sounds grim, doesn't it? Why, then, are we a nation that continues to smoke, drink, and use pills of all kinds, making it appear a pleasing and sophisticated habit for the young? Because most of us simply don't believe that the warnings, no matter how grisly or detailed, apply to us. But may I assure you that no person who becomes a prisoner of the smoking or drinking habit is immune from the slow destruction that will be unleashed upon his body.

Concerning these matters, the Lord, Himself, gave the best warning through a modern prophet, a warning given before the medical studies concerning harmful substances were made. He said, "And again, tobacco [and strong drink or unprescribed drugs] is not for the body, neither for the belly, and is not good for man, but is an herb for bruises and all sick cattle, to be used with judgment and skill" (D&C 89:8). Could there be a more direct and simple statement? If we take no other warning, surely we must at least take this one.

Arthur Gordon tells of a wise doctor who for years worked with individuals addicted to many forms of drugs. The doctor made this comment: "The two saddest words in any language are *if only*—if only I had been wiser—if only I had done it differently—or not done it at all. If only I had used more self-control—if only I hadn't given in the first time. The trouble with 'if only,' " he said, "is that it doesn't change anything."

Well, what's the remedy?

He says strike out the words "if only" and substitute the phrase "next time." That's right. As long as a person keeps saying "if only," he's in trouble. But when he says "next time," we know he is on his way to overcoming his problem.

A great man once wrote: "All of life's experiences are to be either enjoyed or learned from." The hurts and sorrows that we feel in life are not punishments from God; they are messages given by a loving Father who is showing us exactly where we need to change in order to grow into the serenity that is our nature. Understanding this truth entirely changes the way we look at our difficulties.

Chapter 13

Cents and Sensibility

One comedian quipped that the space program was having a little trouble with the astronauts. It seems they wanted to get paid by the mile!

Well, like our mythical astronauts, we all want a lot out of life, and there's nothing really wrong with that as long as we want the right things. We want to develop talents, to become scholars, to lift others' lives, to make it back to the Lord, all of which are noble goals, but unfortunately much of our wanting in modern society gets caught up in material things.

One man said: "My daughter just bought one of those all-inclusive home entertainment units. It has a 25-inch TV set, an AM-FM radio, a turntable and amplifier with six speakers, a digital clock and a light-show projector. To run it, you don't even need batteries. You just plug it into Hoover Dam.'' (In *Reader's Digest*, March 1977, p. 148.)

Yes, in our world we've learned to value and seek after many of the things that money can buy. And if we haven't whipped up a desire for something, we soon will as we are bombarded with hundreds of ads every day telling us how to look better, feel better, smell better, and have more fun. Every magazine shows us pictures of homes that are better decorated than ours. We feel like life won't be complete until we take a cruise or see the world. We'd like to buy a summer home, go on a dream vacation, put a swimming pool in the backyard.

But most of all, we'd just like to pay our bills every month. We'd like to feel secure and unafraid. We'd like to just once go grocery shopping without always calculating the cost of every item.

Coming or going, our hearts are easily snagged on material things. If we are rich, we have to worry about keeping our money, and if we are poor (and who isn't these days?), we are always worried about where it's going to come from. In fact, all of us who feel that hot breath of inflation on our heels may find that our financial security is never far from our minds.

If there is one lesson that we should have learned from all this, it is that everything in life has its cost. If we want to travel one hundred miles in our car, we pay for it, oh, how we pay for it! If we want to have the fanciest home in the flossiest neighborhood, there is a price to pay. Everything in life has its price. Did you ever stop to think what it might cost if you were bent on a life of material well-being? Interestingly, we may find that if we slip into materialism, we pay for our material comforts twice—once in dollars and cents and once in a mind that loses sight of its higher goals.

Jacob, the brother of Nephi, said, "Wo unto the rich, who are rich as to the things of the world. . . . Their hearts are upon their treasures; wherefore, their treasure is their god. And behold, their treasure shall perish with them also." (2 Nephi 9:30.) Now, Jacob is not saying here that it is always wrong to be rich. In fact, those with means who are at the same time spiritually oriented and caring of others are a blessing to the Lord. What is wrong is to have hearts that are continually set upon worldly treasures—treasures bound to vanish with time—and that can be a failing of both the rich and the poor.

It is the failing of the man who begins to look at people only in terms of what they can do for him. Every relationship is looked at in mathematical terms—will it add up to something for me? Instead of seeking to lift others and give them hope for another day, he is only concerned with lifting himself. He may not mean to be selfish, but after all, he thinks, is there really anything wrong with getting paid for the hours spent helping somebody else?

Materialism may be the failing of the workaholic. It is certainly noble to work and achieve some fine thing with our lives, but the nobility tarnishes if we do it at the expense of our families. The man who is greeted by his wife with a flippant, "Hi, stranger," had better think again what success in life he really wants. Sloan Wilson, who wrote *The Man in the Gray Flannel Suit*, had an opportunity at one time to get together a committee of the biggest "big shots to do something nice for public education." He worked with these men for four years, admiring them, studying them, wondering if he could be like them. Included on the committee were the heads of universities and giant corporations. He tried desperately to discover their secrets for career success. It wasn't that they were particularly more brilliant than others. He noticed that one or two had "charm, but so did plenty of second-rate salesmen [he] knew." And some of them were "simply glum." Finally he concluded that they had tremendous energy, energy that enabled them to stay up all night writing a speech, catch a plane across the country to go to a big meeting, and still look forward to the items listed on their daily calendars.

They were totally caught up in their "problem-solving lives" and in wielding their empires. But few could take time for their families. It was a rare man among them who had time for a private life, a long walk with a daughter or son, a lazy chat with his wife. Were these men just bent on making money? Probably not, but they suffered from the kind of materialism that places all of its eggs in the career basket, in the here and now, in the tangible. As Sloan Wilson put it, "they were success junkies." (See "Do Women Really Want That Gray Flannel Suit?" *Deseret News*, 17 April 1980, sec. C, p. 1.)

It's the kind of success that is so easily measurable. It is the lure of materialism that says, "See, I am bigger. I am better. I am more powerful." Compare Wilson's committee study with the following account, appearing in a Dear Abby column, of a fifteen-year-old girl.

"A great man died today. He wasn't a world leader or a famous doctor or a war hero or a sports figure or a business tycoon. But he was a great man. He was my father.

"He didn't get his picture in the paper for heading up committees. I guess you might say he was a person who never cared for credit or honors. He did corny things—like pay his bills on time, go to church on Sunday, and hold an office in the PTA.

"He helped his kids with their homework and drove his wife to the shopping center to do the grocery buying on Thursday night. He enjoyed hauling his kids and their friends to and from football games. He enjoyed simple things—a picnic in the park, country music, mowing the grass, and running with the dog.

"Tonight is the first night of my life without him. I don't know what to do with myself so I am writing to you. I am sorry for the times I didn't show him the proper respect. But I am thankful for many things.

"I am thankful because God let me have him for 15 years. And I am thankful that I was able to let him know how much I loved him. He died with a smile on his face. He knew he was a success as a husband and a father, a son, a brother, and a friend. I wonder how many millionaires can say that. Thanks for listening. You've been a great help! (Signed) His daughter."

It was the comedian Eddie Cantor who said, "A man will spend a whole week figuring out what stocks to buy with three hundred dollars. But he won't spend an hour with his child, in whom he has a greater investment."

Michael Maccoby had this lure in mind when he noted that "from the moment a person starts treating his life as a career, worry is his constant companion. . . . Careerism results not only in constant anxiety, but also in an underdeveloped heart. . . . The careerist constantly betrays himself, since he must ignore idealistic, compassionate, and courageous impulses that might jeopardize his career." (Quoted by Hugh W. Nibley in "Patriarchy and Matriarchy," chapter 5 in *Old Testament and Related Studies* [Salt Lake City: Deseret Book Co. and F.A.R.M.S., 1986], pp. 112–13.)

The lure of materialism is strong. Everything about it reeks of power and pleasure. We like to be able to weigh our significance. It seems that it will make up for the sense of inadequacy that everyone carries in one hidden corner or another of his soul. We like to be able to assure ourselves that we are successful. And the lure may be all the more tantalizing for those who find it always just beyond their grasp.

But this time of economic duress may finally teach us, if we are truly wise, that happiness has no real connection to our bank balance. Those who have been living with the thought that they will be happier tomorrow when they have more have been fooling themselves. Tomorrow arrives and looks oddly the same as today, even if our purses are heavier. Nothing changes if we don't change. With a right economy, the necessities of today may seem like tomorrow's luxuries. And instead of worrying and counting the cost of what we cannot have, let us look around and reflect that the only things we can take with us into eternity are our own souls. Every material possession will be left behind.

I close with this reminder from an unidentified author:

The Things He Didn't Do

He did a lot of clever things,
    Which brought him wealth and fame,
He earned the cheers which conquest brings,
    The public knew his name;
But still they doubted his success
    Who lived with him and knew,
They needed for their happiness
    The things he didn't do.

He never wandered with his boy,
    Or shared a day with him;

He never went for simply joy
    To hunt or fish or swim;
Severe and stern he went his way,
    And never seemed to guess
That they were hungering day by day
    To share his happiness.

They missed him from their home at night
    And longed to see him there,
But fame and fortune held him tight
    And called him from his chair;
And though they gloried in his deeds,
    They sadly came to find
That even earthly greatness needs
    The simple things and kind.

Success is more than pomp or skill,
    And more than worldly fame,
'Tis not enough to climb the hill,
    Or win the passing game;
And who would come to happiness
    Where love and peace are known,
Must learn that none achieves success
    By cleverness alone.

Chapter 14

Courtesy Behind the Wheel

Isn't it funny that when you're a teenager you can hop behind the wheel of a car and be so positive that an accident will never happen to you? And then twenty-five years later when you're the parent of a teenager you're sure that every siren you hear is for your child who has had an accident in your car. That must be part of what the generation gap is all about.

Time does change your perspective. I remember reading of a young married couple whose car was totally demolished when a drunk driver crossed three lanes of traffic and hit them broadside. By some miracle the two were saved, but the car was so far gone they couldn't even open the doors to get out. While they were waiting for help, a little eight-year-old boy came to the window, raised up on tiptoes, and said, "Don't worry, I'll save you." How great is the opti-

mism of youth! You will note that success is more attitude than aptitude.

The thing that can save many of us from the tragedy of automobile accidents is the realization that
each of us as drivers has the capacity to inflict injury
on others, and that capacity is magnified enormously
when behind the wheel of a ton-and-a-half object
moving fifty miles an hour through space. When we
are discourteous or careless as individuals, we can
cause some pain. But when we are careless as motor-
ists, we can cause death or injury that can ruin the
lives of untold numbers. Someone has reminded us
that watching the scenery instead of the car ahead is
the way to become a part of both.

"In a debate on violence in society in the British
House of Lords a few years ago, a member pointed
out to the assembled peers that they each ran a dozen
times more risk of death or injury from auto accidents
than from all other forms of aggression.

"In its brief history of existence, the motor vehicle
has killed or maimed more people than any bomb or
firearm ever invented." (*Royal Bank of Canada Newsletter,* vol. 59, no. 5, May 1978.)

The tragedy of this is that it does not need to be
that way. Most of us believe that automobile accidents are unavoidable, but that is simply not the case.
Most of the bloodshed and carnage on the road is due
to the refusal of drivers to respect the rights of others.
The Royal Bank of Canada pointed out in their
monthly newsletter that most automobile accidents
happen in fair weather and under good road condi-
tions. Some are a result of willful disobedience of the
law. Some happen because a driver knowingly
travels in a car that is dangerously defective. But in
most cases human error is at work.

Now, why bother you with all this? You're probably a very good driver. Do you know that in a study

conducted in the United States nine-tenths of the people rated themselves as "above average" in driving skills and knowledge of safety rules? (*Royal Bank of Canada Newsletter,* May 1978.)

But no matter how great we think we are, sometimes something funny happens to us when we get behind the wheel of a car. It's the same kind of thing that happened to Dr. Jekyll when he drank his magic potion and became the evil Mr. Hyde. We change. Our good nature seems to disappear. The courteous, affable person on the sidewalk suddenly becomes a demon on wheels. I think children learn more insults when their parents are driving than are found in the dictionary of abuse.

I've even seen people sit at a church meeting talking about loving their neighbor. They say warm good-byes and leave with the resolve to be a better person. And what happens? They get behind the wheel of a car to get out of the church parking lot and suddenly it's every man for himself.

The problem is compounded when we're late to go some place. Suddenly we resent the driver in front of us who is going too slow for our taste. "C'mon, c'mon," we say. "Why don't you hurry up, you. . . ?" And that sentence is usually ended with an insulting label. At every intersection we're sure we could have made the turn faster, hit the accelerator sooner. In fact, you've probably heard the definition of a split second: It's that point of time after the light turns green and before the horn in back of you begins honking. (MacGregor's Law states that the first one to see a traffic light turn green is the second car back.)

Why is it that getting behind the wheel brings out our hidden tensions, our worst personalities? Why is it that someone who would never think of cutting in in a grocery line cuts in front of another car for the last parking spot? Surely part of it is because in a car we feel anonymous, a little less responsible for our behavior. Why, if we are discourteous on the road, who's to know? Thank heavens our names or positions in life aren't printed on our license plates!

A college-age girl was traveling along the outside lane of a four-lane highway when suddenly she noticed that up ahead her lane was blocked by a stalled car. She kept trying to ease into another lane, but the car behind her in that lane just wouldn't let her in. Finally in anger, she turned around and shook her fist and yelled an insult. Who was the driver of the offending car? Her fiancé, who got a good laugh out of seeing just how his sweetheart responded under pressure. I'll bet he thought he'd found a worm in the flower. And, of course, she was hopelessly chagrined to have her good image smudged.

As a driver or as a person who travels through the seventy or so years of mortality, it is well to remember that you are never really anonymous. You may be in a crowd of people you'll never see again. You may wear a mask and feel quite hidden. Or you may be driving an automobile when you're late to go some place important to you. But there is always someone watching. You are and the Lord is—the two people whose high opinion you value most in the world. And if you hurt anyone in any way you cannot help but hurt yourself.

In a piece entitled "Not a Sparrow Shall Fall . . . ," Aubrey Tidey tells that when he was eleven his father gave him an air gun. His first victim was a thrush, and though he was elated at his marksmanship, he felt guilty. Later he found his father removing flies and insects from a spider's web and putting them into a matchbox.

"What are you doing, Daddy?" he asked.

"Come with me and I'll show you," he replied. He led the way to the garden and showed him a nest of four young birds with wide-open, hungry mouths. Early the next morning, his father came into his room. In his hand was the body of one of the birds.

"It died during the night," he said. That evening they found another one dead. And a few mornings later he brought in the third body.

"That last one's a sturdy looking little fellow," his father said. "Looks as though he might try out his wings pretty soon."

And to Aubrey the little bird's living to fly became the most important thing in the world. When the day came that the little thing finally tried its wings, it sat on a branch, fluttered, and then dropped to the ground. Its legs kicked once—and it was dead.

"Oh, Daddy," Aubrey cried remorsefully, "it's all my fault. I killed his mother."

"I know, son," said the father. "I saw you do it. Don't worry about it—it was a thing most normal boys have done. But I just wanted you to see how impossible it is to hurt anything or anybody without hurting others—even perhaps the ones who love you. And so often you yourself are the one who is hurt most." (Excerpted with permission from " 'Not a Sparrow Shall Fall . . .' " from "Children Can be Taught Life," *Reader's Digest*, January 1943, pp. 128-29. Copyright © 1942 by The Reader's Digest Assn., Inc.)

From some hidden wellspring of your soul, find the restraint, the tolerance, the self-control to treat everyone with courtesy, whether you know them or not. And make that doubly true when you are behind the wheel of a car that has a hideous potential for hurting the lives of others. Remember what a sign

outside a little town in Japan says, "Please drive carefully. Our children might be disobeying us."

The Lord said it so simply, "Whatsoever ye would
that men should do to you, do ye even so to them"
(Matthew 7:12).

Chapter 15

"Everybody Does It"

We live in a society that has come to believe in and accept fashionable dishonesty. The attitude seems to be that life is so tough you might as well get a break where you can. In fact, many people think that a little dishonesty is not bad. It's just getting caught that hurts. After all, everybody does it.

That's what six-year-old Bobby learned. He and his dad were sitting by the phone one day when it rang and Bobby answered. "Tell them I'm not home, Bobby," his dad said. And at Bobby's puzzled look, his dad said, "It's OK. Everybody does it."

At ten, Bobby was at a restaurant with his mom and dad when Mom caught sight of a little cream pitcher that she wanted which was sitting on their table. "I'll never find another one just like that," she said as she stuck it in her purse. "It's all right, Bobby," his mother said. "Everybody does it."

When Bobby was thirteen, his Uncle Dick let him drive the car whenever they went places together. Bobby didn't have his license yet, and Uncle Dick kept an eagle eye out for the cops, but they never got caught. Bobby wasn't worried about driving without his license because Uncle Dick had assured him that "everybody does it."

At eighteen and as a freshman in college, Bobby (now Bob) was having a hard time in school. He was a great athlete, but getting good grades was something else again. He got used to looking over his shoulder in his exams and getting the answers from somebody else. Other students did the same thing, so Bob didn't feel too bad about it. It just seemed that "everybody did it."

Bob finally made the big time as a football player. One night somebody approached him and offered him big money if he would help to throw the game. The temptation was too much and Bob did it. But he was found out, and his name was spread across all the newspapers for his dishonest deed. Mom and Dad were shocked. Uncle Dick was speechless, and all his fellow cheaters admitted to themselves that they were disappointed. After all, throwing a football game just isn't something that people do.

But whether everybody does it or not, dishonesty is still the same. Fashionable or not, it is immoral. We like to make mental categories and say this is gray and this is dark gray. We like to pretend that we can lie a little, cheat a little, and that there is safety in numbers. We're safe because lying is something that we all do. That is not true.

In stepping beyond the line of honesty, even in what we might fool ourselves into thinking are small ways, we are teaching ourselves and our children unforgettable lessons in crime. One can become a thief as easily over stealing a dime from a pop machine as from stealing thousands from the local bank. It's easy to be shocked when we learn that a national firm has bribed a foreign company for its business, but not blink an eye when we see a shelf full of books that we've borrowed from other people and never returned. In small ways or big ones, dishonesty corrupts us. It takes its toll upon both our own character and our national life. It teaches us that there are no sacred boundaries in life beyond which we may not step.

How many take undeserved deductions on their income taxes? How many cover themselves with excuses instead of admitting to a questioner that they haven't done the job? How many borrow things and never return them? How many speed and then curse when they get caught? These are all forms of dishonesty that eat away at our moral fiber. No matter what everybody else is doing, we cannot guide our actions by the fog of public consensus, but only by the clear light of truth.

To demonstrate its support for honesty, one community, Montello, Wisconsin, annually observes May 2 as "Truth Day" in honor of a little boy named Emmanuel Dannen, who had the courage to stand by his convictions. His story is not a happy one, however. He immigrated to America with his parents in 1845, but two years later they were both dead, leaving him a homeless, four-year-old waif. An uncle saved the small lad from being put up for adoption, but in a little more than a year the uncle died, too. Finally, it seems, luck had turned his way when Samuel Norton and his wife adopted the little boy.

But at the age of eight, Emmanuel chanced, according to local sources, to witness his stepparents murdering a peddler. The Nortons, realizing he had seen the whole event, commanded him to lie to the police. The boy refused, and the enraged Samuel Norton hung him by his wrists from the rafters of their crude log cabin. Again and again the man beat him with willow switches. But the youngster cried, "Pa, I will not lie." Two hours of brutal beating failed to break the spirit of Emmanuel Dannen. Over and over he repeated the fateful words, "Pa, I will not lie." Finally, the boy cried feebly, "Pa, I'm just so cold—" and he collapsed . . . death had ended his ordeal. He had died because he would not lie.

For killing Emmanuel, Samuel Norton and his wife served seven years in prison. But the community's feelings were strong for the boy who would not lie. Indignant citizens raised $1,100 toward the erection of a monument to him. A professional secretary was employed to tour the East to raise additional funds. But he never succeeded in adding a penny to the fund; and when he turned in the bill of expenses, it ironically amounted to $1,100, the exact amount earlier raised by the community.

For over a hundred years, Emmanuel Dannen's grave remained unmarked. But the people of nearby Montello, Wisconsin, did not forget. On May 2, 1954, two thousand people gathered to dedicate a handsome, six-foot, red granite monument erected beside the long-neglected grave. The inscription on it read, "Blessed are they which are persecuted for righteousness' sake: for theirs is the kingdom of heaven."

Consider these two less-dramatic true stories of honesty:

These days when money-grubbing, contract-jumping, and other forms of greed seem rampant in sports, Tom Kite sets a refreshing example of honesty.

Mr. Kite is a professional golfer who was playing in the Hall of Fame Golf Classic at Pinehurst, North Carolina. It was the last round, and Tom Watson, one of the pro tour's best, was leading. A few others, including Tom Kite, were challenging him for the fifty-thousand-dollar prize.

On the fifth hole, Mr. Kite missed a fifteen-foot putt that would have given him a birdie—that is, a score of one under par for the hole. He was left with a six-inch putt, a routine shot. But as he stepped up to the ball, he inadvertently touched it with his club, and it moved less than a quarter of an inch.

Only Mr. Kite saw it, but the golfer's code of ethics left him with just one thing to do. He called a stroke's penalty on himself. As it turned out, one stroke was Tom Watson's margin of victory. Had Tom Kite kept quiet about his minuscule error on the fifth hole, he would have had a tie and a play-off round, with a chance for victory and top money.

Inwardly, though, he would have known differently, and doubtless it would have lain heavy on his conscience. Needless to say, not all other golfers are as strict with themselves. But the integrity of the game depends in large measure on the honesty of those who can be depended upon to report truly on what they did—or didn't do—when no one else was close enough to check up on them. Tom Kite is not as rich today as he might have been, but he can sleep the sound sleep of the just.

It was a crucial game between two small rival high schools. Both towns had turned out to the ballpark. A runner rounded third and headed for home with the tying run. The play at the plate was close and the umpire shouted, "Safe."

But as the runner picked himself up and dusted

himself off, he said, "No, sir, I'm out. I was only a fraction of a second late, but the ball beat me and I was out—fairly."

The crowd was divided in what to think, and for a while there was confusion.

A month later, after graduation time, the young man was called to the office of the president of the local bank. "You have a position here, beginning right now," the bank president said.

"But I wasn't even planning on applying for work here. Who gave my name as a reference?" replied the boy.

"Nobody!" was the answer. "I saw that game a month ago. I knew you and your teammates wanted to win. For a moment I was startled at the outcome of that play at home plate. I had agreed with the umpire. I believe that that day I was the only person at the game who made up his mind as to what he wanted. I wanted you and that kind of honesty in my bank."

We are always stirred by stories like these of courage, integrity, and uncompromising honesty. And we like to think that if we were in the same place we would do as well. We like to think of ourselves as the stars of a high drama, wearing white hats and standing up against all the bad guys. But in reality, we have battles that are just as intense. They are the little ones, and we lose them if we give in to the small dishonesties which we pass off by saying that "everybody does it." Because they do not robe themselves dramatically, because they may not even announce themselves as a test of honesty, we overlook them and tell ourselves that we are doing just fine. Who would dare call us dishonest?

But maybe like the people of Montello, Wisconsin, once in a while we need to celebrate a "Truth Day."

We need to comb through our past and see if there is a dealing that we are not proud of; we need to see if some long-standing debt is unpaid; we need to check through our bookshelf, our toolbox, our kitchen cupboards to see if there are items not returned. We need to commit ourselves to the idea once again that total, absolute, perfect honesty is what we are working for. It doesn't matter what everybody else does. That we may all have the courage to be that honest is my hope.

PART III

Doing

Chapter 16

No Deposit, No Return

A lovely woman sat in a chair at a beauty shop waiting for the beautician to do her hair. The beautician suggested a new style with her hair pulled away from her face and piled high on her head. "That hairstyle would show my ears," the woman replied in disgust. "I hate my ears. They're way too big."

"They are?" answered the beautician. "Whatever gave you that idea?"

"My father told me when I was a child," said the woman. "One day I was looking at a baby and commented what funny ears she had, and my father said, 'You have a lot of room to be talking about ears, Dumbo.' I've never forgotten that comment, and I've hated my ears ever since."

Norman M. Lobsenz wrote of the following experience: "A successful Los Angeles attorney recalls that when he was fourteen, a cousin invited him to spend part of his summer vacation in New York. 'I was thrilled because I'd never been that far away from home before,' the man said. 'But my mother said I couldn't go off on my own—that I'd get on the wrong plane or lose my ticket or get sick. I remember her exact words, "You're just helpless without me to look after you." I *knew* that wasn't true, but she made me *feel* so incompetent I figured she was probably right. And you know something,' the attorney confided, 'every time I start on a trip I get butterflies in my stomach; I still think I'm going to do something wrong or stupid.' " ("How to Give and Get More Emotional Support," *Woman's Day*, September 20, 1977, p. 73.)

It doesn't take much to chip away at another's self-esteem, does it? A thoughtless remark here, a careless word there may leave an emotional scar even when we didn't intend it. We are always so careful to see that our children and loved ones are protected from bodily injury. We don't want them to get broken bones or cuts or bruises, but you know, most broken bones and cuts and bruises heal without leaving a scar at all. They vanish without leaving a trace. But words can mark our personalities in ways we never completely get over. We store them in a memory bank and use them as data in considering all future events. "My ears are too large for that hairstyle," said the woman. "I still think I'm going to do something stupid when I travel," said the attorney.

As Dr. Honor Whitney said, "A constant stream of negative remarks—sarcasm, doubts, rebuffs, putdowns—cut emotional scars into even the sturdiest ego." In fact, she put together a "Self-Image Reinforcement inventory" to examine the comments that people remembered hearing most often in their lives. It consisted of one hundred negative comments and one hundred positive ones. People taking the test checked the comments which they recalled hearing the most as children. Interestingly enough, nine out of every ten remembered hearing, "How many times do I have to tell you . . . ?" frequently in their lives. Beyond that these were the negative comments checked most often:

"Do you expect me to believe *that?*"
"Look at you . . . you're a mess!"
"When are you going to grow up?"
"Can't you do *any*thing right?"
"Now, if *that* wasn't a stupid thing to do!"
"I guess I just can't trust you."
"You're a bad boy (girl)."

To make matters worse, the results of the test showed that two-thirds of these image-destroying phrases were hurled at respondents by parents or siblings. Are they part of your vocabulary? (See Lobsenz, "Emotional Support," pp. 73, 148.)

You know, it's easy for any of us to be gracious to strangers. We try to remember to say, "Thank you, you did a wonderful job," to those whom we meet in social settings. But it is sometimes in the home, where we need most to give emotional support, that we forget to do so. Our nerves get stretched. We're frazzled. In a moment of crisis we forget the power of our words, and suddenly we're saying, "That was stupid," "You're sloppy," or something worse. And the thing that is saddest about this is that these phrases are contagious. Soon everyone in the family has caught them and is disparaging one another. Through these words and phrases we learn in subtle ways to dislike ourselves and to wonder if other people are worth much either. The inaccurate phrases "You *never* . . ." or "You *always* . . ." can become as habitual as brushing our teeth in the morning.

Now, I don't think any of these things are said with malice. "Most of us are simply unaware of how negative our words are," said Dr. Whitney. In fact, as she points out, it doesn't even take words to diminish the self-esteem of those closest to us; a sigh, a scowl, a look of disgust may do it. (See Lobsenz, "Emotional Support," p. 148.) One woman said that when her husband comes home and leaves his clothes over chairs she feels he is saying, "Your work isn't important to me."

So how do we break out of a spiral of negativism that seems to go on and on? More important, how can we turn those powerful words of ours into a support in the lives of others, particularly our families? We've all seen in rural towns those weathered barns that have taken such a beating that they sag. How can we avoid having the same effect on our families?

Let me give you three ideas that may help:

First of all, it is difficult to support others if you are hurting yourself. No one can quench his thirst from your empty cup. In fact, as Norman Lobsenz observes in his article, "insecure people have a psychological need to put others down" as a means of feeling strong themselves ("Emotional Support," p. 148). We must learn to think positively about ourselves without demeaning others in the process. Then we must develop ourselves to be worthy of our positive thoughts.

In some ways and in spite of their many and obvious differences, there is still very little difference in people. However, that little difference makes a big difference. The little difference is attitude. The big difference is whether that attitude is positive or negative.

Family counselor Dr. Thomas C. McGinnis said, "If you always find yourself apologizing, you can be sure somebody once impressed on you that you were not very important. If you always find yourself asking for advice, you know somebody once convinced you your judgment was not to be trusted." (In Lobsenz, "Emotional Support," p. 150.)

Feeling good about yourself is not one of life's luxuries; it is a necessity if we are ever to help others.

Second, we must recognize that we are important in the lives of others. I wonder, for instance, if any parent ever truly understands how vital he is in the lives of his children. And a child exhibits his need by the clinging onto skirts or tugging at the suit coat, the coming in to parents at night to crawl into bed, the calling for advice even when a grown son or daughter. To a child of any age a parent's estimation of him carries him back to his first ideas about who he is, whether he is an important and vital person or not. In a different way, each of us is an important somebody to somebody else.

Third, we must train ourselves to notice the good things in others. All of us have them! Faults and weaknesses cause us annoyance, so it's easy to notice them. But in the meantime positive qualities may pass unnoticed.

We may have to watch more carefully, exercise more patience, and overlook some behaviors before discovering even small strengths. But when inevitably they are found, if they are sincerely, obviously, and openly appreciated, they can be stepping stones to another person's heightened sense of good and worth in himself. And often this is the only thing that will motivate him to rise above the negative. William

James observed that the greatest discovery of his generation was that human beings *can* alter their lives by altering their attitudes of mind. Remember, your altitude will determine your attitude.

Giving emotional support to our loved ones through the use of positive, uplifting, and encouraging words and expressions is the deposit. The return is the growth of souls, including our own. Conversely, no deposit, no return—for anyone!

Instead of allowing our special loved ones to be caught in a world of negatives, let's buoy them up to face each day. Let's recognize how powerful our words are and give them as gifts to the lives of others.

Chapter 17

Think Before Acting

The story is told of the important executive of a large manufacturing plant who was known as a rather reserved, quiet, but very efficient operator. One day one of his factory superintendents who urgently needed his counsel was told by his secretary that he was "in conference" and was not to be disturbed. "But how can he be in conference?" exclaimed the superintendent, an impetuous sort of man. "One of the other employees told me he was alone, and I must see him on a matter of great importance." With that he pushed by the secretary, even after she said, "You may come back in a few moments, but at present he is not to be disturbed." Without knocking, he abruptly opened the door to the executive's private office. After a glance into the office, he quickly and quietly closed the door, and with much embarrassment faced the secretary and said, "Why—why, he is on his knees!"

"Yes, in conference, as I told you," said the secretary.

"I—I'm sorry. I didn't know he was that sort of man," apologized the superintendent; "guess the one in there with him is of greater importance than I am." As he left, he still carried an amazed look on his face.

Many years ago I learned the importance of taking time each morning to be in conference with the Lord and to just ponder.

Nephi said: "For my soul delighteth in the scriptures, and my heart pondereth them, and writeth them for the learning and the profit of my children."

He continues: "Behold, my soul delighteth in the things of the Lord; and my heart pondereth continually upon the things which I have seen and heard." (2 Nephi 4:15–16.)

As I have observed the lives of others and have reflected on my own experiences, I have concluded that it is very easy for the mechanical and mundane to take precedence over higher priorities. A little time each day just to be alone to think, pray, and plan can make such a difference in how a day turns out, and that time is not easy to find in our present-day society of instant TV watching, hurry-up, helter-skelter, meet-the-schedule demands. We desperately need quiet moments to let our minds relax and to get our thoughts organized more effectively.

I think of a politician who, during a recent election, was engaged in a hard-fought, fast-moving campaign. He found himself rushing from speech to speech, busily defending and countering the many charges made against him. One day as he was hurrying out of his office, a campaign worker caught him in the hall.

"What do you think of the situation now?" the worker asked.

"Don't bother me," said the candidate rushing by. "I've got to make a speech. This is no time to think." That seems to sum up the plight of so many of us. There is just not time to think.

However, contrast the politician's attitude and response with that of these two enterprising youngsters who sought counsel and were real thinkers:

The two boys set up a lemonade stand in front of their home. Late in the afternoon they were becoming very discouraged because they had made only one sale. "What can we do to improve sales?" one of the boys asked his dad.

"Well," his father replied, "think about how other businesses promote. Use your imaginations and creativity."

Two hours later, the boys came into the house grinning from ear to ear. "You were right, Dad. We listened to what you said, and it worked. We sold out!"

Pleasantly surprised that his advice had turned their business around, the father asked, "How did you do it, boys? What kind of a gimmick did you use?"

"We decided to do like the grocery stores and give away stamps," one boy replied.

"Stamps? Where in the world did you get stamps?"

"Out of your postage box," the boys said. "We gave away two full rolls!"

By reserving some quiet time each day we can avoid all kinds of mistakes and eliminate unnecessary blunders. We are able to weigh our choices carefully. We can contemplate our options. In doing so, we discover our own potential and commit ourselves to do better.

Samuel T. Whitman has written a classic story of yesteryear entitled "Forgotten Wedges" which illustrates so well our tendency to act sometimes without thinking. The results can often be sad and costly.

"The story of the iron wedge began many years ago when the white-haired farmer was a lad on his father's homestead. The sawmill had then only recently been moved from the valley, and the settlers were still finding tools and odd pieces of equipment scattered about. . . .

"On this particular day, it was a faller's wedge —wide, flat, and heavy, a foot or more long, and splayed from mighty poundings. The path from the south pasture did not pass the woodshed; and, because he was already late for dinner, the lad laid the wedge . . . between the limbs of the young walnut tree his father had planted near the front gate. He would take the wedge to the shed right after dinner, or sometime when he was going that way.

"He truly meant to, but he never did. It was there between the limbs, a little tight, when he attained his manhood. It was there, now firmly gripped, when he married and took over his father's farm. It was half grown over on the day the threshing crew ate dinner under the tree. . . . Grown in and healed over, the wedge was still in the tree the winter the ice storm came.

"In the chill silence of that wintry night, with the mist like rain sifting down and freezing where it fell, one of the three major limbs split away from the trunk and crashed to the ground. This so unbalanced the remainder of the top that it, too, split apart and went down. When the storm was over, not a twig of the once-proud tree remained.

"Early the next morning, the farmer went out to mourn his loss. 'Wouldn't have had that happen for a thousand dollars,' he said. 'Prettiest tree in the valley, that was.'

"Then, his eyes caught sight of something in the splintered ruin. 'The wedge,' he muttered reproachfully. 'The wedge I found in the south pasture.' A glance told him why the tree had fallen. Growing edge-up in the trunk, the wedge had prevented the limb fibers from knitting together as they should." (As quoted by Spencer W. Kimball, "Hidden Wedges," *Improvement Era*, June 1966, pp. 523–24.)

I suppose we all can relate to that experience because leaving wedges here and there is human. I have left many wedges around during the course of my life, and quite often they reappear in unusual ways.

Years ago a teacher friend shared this thought with me:

"A time of quietude brings things into proportion and gives us strength. We all need to take time from the busyness of living, even if it be only ten minutes to watch the sun go down or the city lights blossom against a canyon sky. We need time to dream, time to remember, and time to reach the infinite. Time to be."

I have always felt that whenever we are facing situations where there seems to be no way out, we need to look up and listen. The Lord has said: "Hearken, O ye people, and open your hearts and give ear from afar; and listen, you that call yourselves the people of the Lord, and hear the word of the Lord and his will concerning you" (D&C 63:1).

Jesus said, "Who hath ears to hear, let him hear" (Matthew 13:9). Learning to ponder, pray, and listen takes practice. I recall so well the tremendous demands on my time and resources shortly after arriving in the mission field as a new mission president.

There didn't seem to be a single moment to just take care of the essentials in my work or personal life. I decided to spend one hour every morning after our office study class and daily devotional in a private conference with the Lord. I asked my secretary to hold all calls and to protect my privacy. At first I felt almost guilty taking a whole hour to just sit and think, plan, and pray. About the third day, it was amazing how my mind came to rest and a sweet peace seemed to take over. As I planned my day and schedule, making some detailed preparation for talks, interviews, appointments, etc., I was able to seek confirmation from the Lord, and then this was the real discovery and blessing—to just *listen* and *hear* the response. I knew the source from which the inspiration came.

From personal experience I have come to know that we can avoid misplacing wedges if we think before we act. That we may so do is my desire for us all.

Chapter 18

My Father Taught Me

Many thoughts have gone through my mind as I have brought together the feelings, ideas, and subjects for this book. I find it impossible to write on any subject without pondering and reflecting on the influence many people have had on my life, particularly my own father. I often smile at some of his comments and the counsel he gave as I was growing up. For instance:

"You boys always brighten up our home; you never turn off the lights."

"Paul, our neighbors say that one of the great mysteries in life is that you can pitch a no-hitter in a neighborhood baseball game, but as their paperboy you can't hit the front porch with a newspaper."

Or, "Someday science may be able to explain why children can't walk around a mud puddle."

And, "Why is it that all the food kids love to eat is so noisy when they eat it?"

Fathers—our wonderful fathers. How many times has dear ol' Dad been there when money or understanding was needed? And he always seemed to care enough to sit down and give advice or lend his children a listening ear.

Little did Dad realize before he became a father that children tend to be greater loads of responsibility than bundles of joy. Sticky fingers around the neck, greasy handprints on the front of pants, little mouths talking all at once. But miraculously fathers learn to adapt. The knowledge they learn is usually acquired on the firing line—from experience with their children! In spite of this, most men who have some level of responsibility, awareness, patience, and love usually do quite well.

If it weren't for fathers, many children wouldn't have signed up for little league baseball or football, learned how to camp out or to fish—wouldn't have gotten or even been allowed to get dirty.

Then there are the various normal challenges of childhood that fathers have to suffer through. The children might have just gotten over a bout with chicken pox and suddenly the flu bug hit. Their tonsils have had to come out, and somebody has fallen off the slide and has had to have stitches in his head.

And there is always the battle of the budget. It's one new pair of shoes after another, and then the dentist calls to say that the X rays reveal more cavities and subtly asks, "Have you received the bill yet?" It's a hard job, this business of being a father and helping to raise a family. But all things considered, most fathers do a pretty wonderful job.

Nearly two thousand years ago the Apostle Paul reminded the Hebrews that even though their fathers had corrected them on occasion, they still owed them reverence (see Hebrews 12:9). I believe he would counsel our generation today the same way. Do we give reverence to our fathers? Are we not, in fact, in subjection to our fathers? What is a father? What is his role and place in our lives?

These questions could be addressed appropriately to either children or to their fathers. I would like, here, to direct a question to the fathers. Fathers, what would your children answer to, ''What is your father like? Does he love you? How does he show that love?''

A close friend of mine told of a relationship he had with his father. This friend grew up on a farm. His father loved him in a way that might seem almost foreign to a city dweller. You see, this father and son were best friends. They worked together, they played together, and they talked together, much the same as two people of the same age would talk. And yet there was a difference, for the son respected his father in a manner that he never would have respected his peers. His father stood lower by far than the God this young man worshipped, but still he was next to God in the boy's eyes. My friend tells how they would spend hours together in the fields. He particularly remembers how he would spend great portions of time riding on his father's knee while they were on a tractor doing the farm work. Now as he considered what that must have meant in terms of a foot, long since fallen asleep, or leg muscles that must have ached from the weight of a ten- or eleven-year-old son, he winces, and then knows, in a special way, of the love his father had for him.

They talked of things that were trivial, passing things that were important only in the fancy and curiosity of a young boy. Important to him today and totally insignificant tomorrow. But through those seemingly unimportant things, the two were brought to speak of things that held secrets of happiness in life. And through those things that were so salient to life, they were led to other matters that had eternal implications. Their conversations drifted back and forth through these wonderful dimensions of friend-ship, and thus, the father was able to teach his son in a very special and effective way.

Many parents pass up endless opportunities of this kind, for, as with this father and son, it takes time. Hour after hour of seemingly insignificant yet ever-to-be-remembered discussions that are gently and not too liberally sprinkled with the treasures of life and eternity.

Fathers, what are you teaching your sons? And how are you going about that instruction? Do your sons look at you as being the great lawgiver, the judge, the jury, and the executioner? Are you a per-son to be feared and avoided? One to be ignored? Or do they look at you with love and respect and great appreciation?

Do you remember when that first baby was born? Do you recall the pride you felt at knowing you were the father of a child? And now perhaps the most im-portant question of all: Do you remember the prom-ises you made to the child and to yourself or perhaps to the Lord? You were quite visionary in that moment of birth, weren't you? You foresaw what a wonderful young man or what a beautiful young lady this child would grow up to be. And you knew that the great-ness and the beauty would largely be the result of you and your wife's influence, and you promised that that influence would be given with untiring and unrelenting dedication. Almost all fathers are like that in the beginning of their parental experience.

Have you kept those precious promises made in your heart as you looked at that tiny infant cradled in your wife's arms?

There are spaces in a child's life, be the child a boy or girl, that can only be filled by the father, just as there are spaces that only a mother can fill. What is happening to those opportunities that are reserved only for you?

In baseball terms, must it be one of the inevitable facts of life that some fathers continue to have such miserable won-loss records? The pennant is the child, and the outcome of the race is determined by the wins that are accumulated throughout the life of that child while he is with his parents. And every game is important. Too many fathers find themselves in the September of the season trailing by twenty-seven games with only twenty-six games left to play. In layman's terms, that means they can't win. But winning every game isn't the important thing—it's playing every game, and winning a high percentage.

And then come those special days when you will be able to play a double header—have a doubly important opportunity to relate to a child. It doesn't matter then whether you feel like playing or not. The great father will rise to the occasion and work beyond his natural capacity toward something bigger than himself.

I'm thinking of a young man in junior high who became quite accomplished as a Ping-Pong player. There was no other student his age that could beat him. One time a friend grew curious about how he had developed his great ability, so he asked, ''How did you learn to play this game so well?'' With no shame whatsoever—indeed it was quite the opposite —the young teenager replied, ''My father taught me.''

My father taught me! Can you imagine a greater statement made by a son about his father?

Let me tell you how this particular father accomplished this time-consuming feat. Even a game as simple as Ping-Pong takes a great deal of time if one is to become proficient at it. It seems the father and son started playing together when the son was about ten years old. The father could tell that it was going to bore him to death to play against a young person with such limited skill. Then he struck upon an idea —a special flash of inspiration, I suspect.

He explained to his son that the score at the beginning of the game would be 18 to 0 in favor of the boy. It was agreed that each time the boy defeated his father, the boy's score would be lowered one point for the next game, making it 17 to 0 in favor of the boy at the beginning of the next game. A second condition was that anytime the father defeated his son three times in a row the boy's score would be taken up a point.

And so the competition began. Now they both had to play their very best in order to win. It was thrilling and exciting for both of them. Slowly the boy's score began to move downward to begin each new game. The father gave no quarter, and the son was delighted to be granted none; his only reward was a lower beginning score.

Finally one day the son defeated his father and subtracted one point so that the beginning score of the next game was 0 to 0. Still the battle was not over. Now in order to maintain the beginning score for which the son had worked so hard and so long, it was agreed that he would have to beat his father three times in a row. Victory was then mingled with defeat as the father and son struggled back and forth.

The day finally came when the son defeated his father three times in a row. Now they would always be able to play together and really have fun. The boy was destined to become somewhat of a champion. But how important is it to be a Ping-Pong champion? Well, not too many Ping-Pong players are making a hundred thousand dollars a year or signing multi-million-dollar contracts. But something far more important was achieved that no amount of money could represent. The son was able to announce to his friend, "My father taught me!"

There are some other interesting things you should know about this boy. He was not a trouble-maker. He achieved as good grades as his ability allowed. He was honest, well groomed; he found joy in life and had great faith in the life yet to come. He had no idea what it was like to be truant or deviant in his behavior, except in those little things that keep all young boys from perfection. He was a growing and glowing young man.

No doubt many things contributed to his accomplishments, but in all these one of the major factors was that loving, caring influence of a father who was creative and innovative and who devoted his time and efforts to raising up a son who could proudly state, "My father taught me!"

Fathers, let's again ask the question, What am I teaching my son or my daughter? We are teaching them something, for that is an unavoidable fact. But is it for their good or for their detriment? For fathers who fail to teach righteous things to their children there are almost no laws in this life to punish their disregard for parental responsibility.

And for the father who is faithful and dedicated and who is teaching his children by the power of his love and the commitment of his time and effort, there is very little in terms of awards or rewards. Unless, of course, he can take joy in a child's simple little statement, "My father taught me."

Oh, incidentally, it may be of interest to you to know that the father of the Ping-Pong player was the son of the farmer who drove the tractor and had the cramped and aching leg. Does that surprise you?

The scriptures record that the sins of the parents will be upon the heads of the children even unto the third and the fourth generations (see Exodus 20:5). Doesn't it stand to reason, then, that the righteousness of the parents will also be upon the heads of the children, even unto the third and fourth generations, to bless them for all eternity? Think about it. "My father taught me."

Chapter 19

A Father's Role in a Changing World

Many fathers these days feel a little bit like extras waiting in the wings while the family drama unfolds. Most of them want to be involved with their families, but they think they don't have much time. Inflation, resulting in that ever-present need to make another dollar, keeps them running harder and faster for job success. Commuting sometimes an hour or more to work eats up their precious time. One father complained that by the time he gets home from work the smaller children are ready for bed and the older children are so dominated by television that he can't hold a family conversation. "I'm on the outskirts," he says. "The children change and grow and I hardly know them."

Another father said that he would like to have closer and more successful relations with his children, but he finds it difficult in these times. He'd like it to be different, but, he says, "a father can't always direct the family in his own image." (In Kenneth L. Woodward with Phyllis Malamud, "The Parent Gap," *Newsweek*, September 22, 1975, p. 50.) One fellow says that his twelve-year-old summed up present-day family life rather neatly as he left the dinner table: "See you all at the next meal."

We read it in almost every magazine, in last night's newspaper, hear it on television: "The Family Is Obsolete." In our changing world, child rearing is a very difficult task—for some, seemingly impossible. As John Anderson, a director for the Family Service of Detroit, said, "Parents have lost control over their families. They feel inadequate, overwhelmed" (in Woodward, "Parent Gap," p. 48).

And Margaret Mead, a noted anthropologist, said, "We have become a society of people who neglect our children, are afraid of our children, find children a surplus instead of the [reason for] living" (in Woodward, "Parent Gap," p. 48).

It's not the things we do each day
That determine victories won;
More often it's things we don't do
And the things we have left undone.

Author Unknown

Are we, the parents of America, going to stand idly by and let the family disintegrate? Are we going to throw up our hands and let the kids come up however they may? Many fathers are letting that happen by default. They are so busy punching clocks or building buildings, that children take last place in their priorities.

A 1975 article in *Newsweek* magazine stated: ''This year, 6 million Americans will take a step that will significantly change their own lives and profoundly affect the next generation: they will have children. How they raise these youngsters will have a greater impact on American society than the way they vote, the technologies they produce, the wars they wage or the art they create.'' (Woodward, ''Parent Gap,'' p. 48.)

Theodore Roosevelt warned: ''Of all the work that is done or that can be done for our country, the greatest is that of educating the body, the mind, and above all the character, giving spiritual and moral training to those who in a few years are themselves to decide the destinies of the nation.'' The destiny of any nation at any given time depends on the opinions of its young men and women under twenty-five.

Fathers, where are your energies really devoted? Are you spending your life's effort, your intellect, your best quality time in your business and giving your family only your tired leftovers? They deserve more than that. They desperately need more than that. The last decade in our country has brought every cherished value into question. Your children have entered a confusing world, a world that assaults them with violence and tension and topsy-turvy ideals. The best experts claim they no longer know for sure what is right or wrong. Your children are exposed to every kind of pressure. They don't know how to act or who to be if they haven't had a parent who has taken the time to teach them a meaningful value system, the gospel of Christ.

That is your obligation, and no one else can do it. Mother can't do it alone. You can't expect schools or peer groups or television—that ''flickering blue parent,'' as psychologist Kenneth Keniston calls it (in

Woodward, "Parent Gap," p. 55)—to assume the responsibility for teaching your children and instilling values. However overwhelming it may be, your role is that of a parent, of a father, and if you are afraid to assume it, your children's behavior and basic beliefs will be left to chance. How many parents grieve over children who have gone astray, saying, "But we gave him everything"? Obviously they had not given him "everything"; they had been too afraid or too busy to teach him values, to guide, to direct, to discipline. In these turbulent times that need has not diminished, it has been enhanced.

Some years ago during a very unpleasant winter, a little paperboy went to his father and asked if he could quit delivering his newspapers. He would get so cold as he rode his bike down the icy roads, and his fingers seemed to freeze as he folded his newspapers and went along his route. His father answered the boy's question with these words: "You may quit in the summer when the sun is shining, but you may not quit now in the snow." Because of this valuable lesson in tenacity and many more just like it taught by his father, this little boy, you will not be surprised to learn, has grown to be a successful business executive, noted for his perseverance and his going on when the going is tough. He gives the credit to his father.

I wonder what would have happened if that same event had been enacted today by a typical father and his son. I can see it now: The boy probably wouldn't even have bothered asking his father if he could quit his paper route in the first place, and if he had, the father would probably have said, "Do your own thing. It's your life—live it!" Or, "If it feels good, it's right." As parents, many of us have become hesitant to assert ourselves, to declare what we believe, and

perhaps have been willing to count on others to influence our children in the higher values.

As we celebrate special occasions like Father's
Day, let us do more than receive our cards and gift-
wrapped ties. Let us sit down with our wives and
define quite specifically what values we need to teach
our children. I know a couple who started with a very
basic list. It said, "We want our children to be honest.
We want our children to learn to work." It went on
like that. After their list was determined, they very
conscientiously looked for teaching moments in
which to instill those values. Children, these parents
discovered, don't just absorb the best values by
osmosis. They must be taught. I have seen many
hardworking couples who have very lazy children because definite work assignments and other responsibilities were not given or made important in their
children's lives. Remember, doing nothing is the
hardest work of all. God gives every bird its food, but
He does not throw it in the nest. Plautus said: "He
who would eat the kernel must first crack the shell."

John Eisenhower, son of the late President Eisenhower, tells this story about his father: "He was a
tough father, always concerned with duty, a strong
man who always played by the rules. There was one
time, though, when we were in Mexico, when he was
caught in the middle. I was 13, and about to go on a
14-mile hike to qualify as a first-class Boy Scout. I
wasn't allowed company, juice or milk, or anything
like that; I had to do it all on my own. The women of
the house started to get on Dad's back, saying, 'How
could you let that boy go alone, what with rattle-
snakes and who knows what else out there!' He
knew I had to do it right, that I would not accept help
—and that he wouldn't offer it. But many years later I
found out that he'd followed me along in the car the

entire distance, staying well out of sight, but being there, in case I got into any real trouble." (In Lynn Minton, comp., " 'To Dad, with Love,' " *Good Housekeeping*, July 1975, p. 87.)

And that's what we have to do as fathers. Teach values, teach strong principles and then follow along just out of sight to help our children face their private hazards.

Ponder this: When a certain national magazine folded, the managing editor was able to catch on with a newspaper. But within a few months the newspaper was purchased by a chain, and in the cost-cutting that followed, the editor found himself out of a job once more. He came home and broke the news to his wife and his three small sons. The wife did her best to comfort him. The three boys stared at him round-eyed.

The next morning the man arose after his boys had left for school, and wandered into his study. In his wastebasket were the remains of three china piggy banks. On his desk was a small pile of quarters, dimes, and nickels. Under the coins was a crudely lettered message. It read, "We believe in you, Pop." Even without knowing the father in this story, it is not difficult to understand the impact he had had on his children as a teacher and a friend.

It takes time and perhaps a rearranging of our priorities, but if we can do these things, it is possible to keep our personal families from disintegrating and ourselves from becoming extras in the family drama, wondering what's happening to our children onstage. We'll be centerstage, caught up in the most important single thing any of us can do in this society —rearing responsible, secure, and happy children. The rewards are tremendous.

It is as someone once wrote:

A Dad's Greatest Job

I may never be as clever as my neighbor down the
    street;
I may never be as wealthy as some other men I meet;
I may never have the glory that some other men have
    had,
But I've got to be successful as a little fellow's Dad.

There are certain dreams I cherish that I'd like to see
    come true;
There are things I would accomplish ere my working
    time is through.
But the task my heart is set on is to guide a little lad,
And make myself successful as that little fellow's
    Dad.

I may never come to glory; I may never gather gold.
Men may count me as a failure when my business life
    is told.
But if he who follows after shall be manly, I'll be
    glad—
For I'll know I've been successful as a little fellow's
    Dad.

It's the one job that I dream of; it's the task I think of
    most.
If I fail that growing youngster, I'd have nothing else
    to boast.
For though wealth and fame I'd gather, all my future
    would be sad,
If I failed to be successful as that little fellow's Dad.

Chapter 20

"To the World's Greatest Dad"

Not long ago Jim Bishop recorded this true incident in his newspaper column.

"The night, it seems, was dark in one of a city's cheaper neighborhoods, when suddenly an ambulance with its blinking light came whining down the streets. It had been summoned to a ramshackle flat where an old man was dying. The sign in front said, 'Furnished Rooms.'

"The intern jumped from the ambulance and bounded up the steps. As he took them two at a time, he noticed the peeling paint, the rancid odor of cooking in the air. The landlady, wringing her hands, let him into an apartment some flights up.

"As the door opened, he saw him—an old man lying on a worn linoleum floor. The room held noth-

ing but a bare table and chest and a single army cot
with a thin mattress.

" 'How long has he been like this?' said the intern as he crouched over the frail body. He noted the
waxen skin, the ribs that showed, the shallow breath-
ing through blue lips.

"The landlady shrugged and a policeman joined
the group. Apparently she'd only seen him to collect
rent. The neighbors were no help. They'd maybe
seen him but didn't know his name. The intern gave
the old man a shot in the curve of his elbow and then
for the policeman's records said, 'Cardiac—and also
malnutrition.'

"The slight body was wrapped in a cotton blanket, bundled onto the stretcher and hurried down the
rickety stairs. The policeman was left to determine
identification.

"This was a skilled cop, a man whose interests
and abilities were better matched to solving crime
than casing out an apartment like this. Nothing unusual here; he'd seen this type of thing before. There
was a bowl with dried cereal stuck to the bottom, a
towel rack. But suddenly he noticed that there on the
dresser stood two photographs, people the poor man
loved.

"The first was a beautiful woman with dark hair
caught up in a twist above her head. On the back of
this photo was a yellowed newspaper clipping an-
nouncing the death of Mrs. Kenneth Keighly, September, 1932. The second photo depicted a man and
two daughters. It seems the old man had been mus-
cular in his youth. His arm was held protectively
around those little girls.

"Gradually, as the policeman searched the room,
the old man's identity emerged. He was Kenneth
Keighly, a compositor for an Ohio newspaper. When
his young wife had died, he'd been left to rear two

daughters alone. The children must have received good educations. A note found there said in case of emergency to notify Mrs. R. K., former superintendent of nurses, or Mrs. P. M., a high school principal.

"On a shelf above the iron cot were the old man's prized possessions—some bronzed infant shoes and a bundle of letters tied together with some string.

"The policeman became interested. He pulled the string and out fell some snapshots—pictures of little girls hugging their dad, important family moments caught on film. And on each picture, printed in a neat hand, were names and birth dates.

"The policeman read the letters. He couldn't help himself. 'Love, Miriam,' they said. 'Kisses, Jane.'

"One letter read, 'It is useless to come here. With my crazy Indians, you would have no privacy. It is best that you stay in Columbus.'

"Another said, 'You're not young anymore and it would be like having a fifth child.'

"Still another, 'Your social security should be more than enough.'

"Across town at the hospital, the ambulance arrived—too late. The stark lights in the hospital corridor revealed the old man's body as limp, lifeless. The intern ordered oxygen in a last minute attempt to save the life. He listened again with his stethoscope —then shook his head. 'He's gone. Whoever starves to death in a big city?'

"The doctor was about to leave when the nurse stopped him. 'I need you here, while I check his clothes for effects,' she said. She found nothing in his trousers. But she did find something in the sweater pocket. She pulled out a little wooden pedestal with a miniature loving cup on top. It said, 'To the World's Greatest Dad.' " ("Starves—Alone," *Roanoke Times*, 1978.)

This is a true account. And while it may have been

highlighted in a newspaper column, I wonder how many times it is repeated across our country. How many people are starving for food or for attention or for affection simply because they committed the crime of growing old? We all get old, after all, one day at a time. It may take you by surprise. A child may come carrying a picture of you and say, ''Who is this?'' And you'll know it's happened. Will you be any different inside? Will you care any less for the love and attention of others? Of course not.

One famous American rabbi said it was curious that one father could take care of twelve children, but twelve children could not take care of one father (Jimmy Carter, address given in the Salt Lake Tabernacle, November 27, 1978). The whole idea of family is to love one another, rejoice in the triumphs, and share the burdens. Certainly parents do that for children. Mothers are awakened in the night at the baby's cry or the toddler's nightmares. Fathers wait up for dating teenagers. Mothers scrape peanut butter off their velvet couches; fathers get dents in their car fenders. Parents are faced with comic books and bills and rock music and phones that are always tied up, and they face it gladly.

Can children when they are grown do any less for parents? Most parents don't demand special care. They just want to know they are still loved and included, that against any odds their family is still there to support them. How many lonely men and women walk out to their mailboxes every day hoping there will be a letter? How many are cooped up in tiny rooms waiting for a visit, an outing?

Ella Wheeler Wilcox wrote:

> They say the world is round, and yet
> I often think it square,

So many little hurts we get
    From corners here and there.
But one great truth in life I've found,
    While journeying to the West—
The only folks we really wound
    Are those we love the best. . . .

We flatter those we scarcely know,
    We please the fleeting guest,
And deal full many a thoughtless blow
    To those we love the best.

("Life's Scars," in Hazel Felleman,
sel., *The Best Loved Poems of the American
People* [Garden City, New York:
Doubleday, 1936], p. 645.)

Most of us with older parents, relatives, or neighbors have good intentions. We really do. We mean to visit them, to take them the first flower of the spring, to light up a weekend with an outing, to read needs even when unspoken. We just don't take time to do it. We tell ourselves we're too busy; we're caught up with mortgage payments, and children's lessons, and appointments that never end. And these may be good things. But sometimes in life the good is the enemy of the best. Just as you would not knowingly let anyone starve to death while you were feasting at a banquet, do not let anyone's life go unnoticed because yours is too full. Especially do not forget your parents who have been mindful of you every day of your life. Remember, your parents are your same age inside, and their wrinkles merely indicate where smiles have been.

The Lord said it simply: "Honor thy father and thy mother."

Chapter 21

Hard Knocks

While I was attending a recent graduation exercise, a new graduate remarked to me: "I've noticed that all things are difficult before they are easy." His comment reminded me of what Immanuel Kant, the philosopher, said: "Man longs to live in comfort and pleasure, but nature, who knows better what he was made for, gives him toil and painful strife so that he may raise himself above the sphere of his sorrows." In a way Kant's statement could well be the motto for the school of hard knocks. It is a difficult old school—this thing that has been known as the "School of Hard Knocks." And I have noticed that few, if any of us, wish to enroll at the freshman level. I once said to a group of young enthusiasts: "Isn't it interesting that we build artificial obstacles on a golf course to make the game more exciting and

challenging, and then complain because of the difficulties that are forced upon us in the game of life?''

Yet through it all we know, if we will only allow
ourselves to admit the fact, that no one ever achieves
anything really interesting to himself or worthwhile
for anyone else, no matter how many college degrees
he may have gained, until he has entered and has
had at least a few courses in the ''University of Hard
Knocks.''

Thomas Edison was once asked what advice he
had for young people. He said: ''Always be interested in whatever you are doing at the time, and
think only of that thing in all its bearings and master
it. Don't mind the clock, but keep at it, and let nature
indicate the necessity of rest. After resting, go at the
work again with the same interest. The world pays
big prices for the people who know the values and
satisfaction of persistent hard work.'' My father put it
this way: ''When your ship comes in, make sure you
are willing to unload it.''

I recall some years ago at graduate school hearing
a lecture given by a famous surgeon whose name was
well known throughout the nation at the time. During his professional career he had picked up quite a
few graduate degrees and several public honors. He
spent a wonderful hour lecturing about good health,
handling his subject in a masterful way. He seemed
to have great empathy for those who were hurt or
sick. Later I asked him if he had not had some serious
illness of his own.

''Yes,'' he said, ''about three years ago I fell from
a ladder while painting a room and broke my back.
For several days, with the exception of a few moments one day, I was unconscious. And for eight
weeks I lay on my back on the most uncomfortable
bed invented by man—a frame that pushed my back

up higher than my head or feet—and during much of that time I was in pain, with an injured pelvic area, three broken ribs, internal injuries, and a broken back."

I said, "That must have been quite an experience, particularly for a doctor."

"Yes," he replied, "but you see I'm all right now. And I am a much better doctor as a result. I have a knowledge of sickness and a sympathy for the patient that I could not have had without this experience in the school of hard knocks."

It seems that each school that I ever attended had its school songs and yells. Perhaps one of the yells for this famous university could be: "Black and blue, blue and black—you hit me, and I'll hit you back. Rah! Rah! Rah!" Silly! Yes, but most college yells are silly when examined critically for real meaning in the words. Perhaps one of the required courses in this school of hard knocks could be "The Give and Take of Life, 101."

Sometimes it requires a struggle on the athletic field, a broken rib, an elbow in the eye, a beanball, torn ligaments, or a sprained ankle. But in the end these kinds of struggles develop physical health and courage in the meeting of life's tasks. Or maybe one must engage in some form of hard, honest labor that tries the body and taxes one's patience almost to the breaking point, yet provides a discipline that is good for the soul.

I remember hearing a leading educator say that one of the best things that could happen to every college graduate would be for him to work for a few years immediately after graduation at some physical labor in order to get the feel of the task and a deeper appreciation for the role that manual labor plays in the world. Perhaps we all do not agree with such an approach, but there is one fact we must recognize: life cannot be learned entirely from a textbook, no matter how fine and comprehensive that book may be.

President David O. McKay once said to me: "Let us realize that the privilege to work is a gift, that power to work is a blessing, that love of work is success."

Someday looking back (I wonder if I dare say it), we will view as a big joke our present system of so-called education, where scores of students sit together taking notes from the expressed ideas of one learned lecturer, later at exam time giving back that information as little changed as possible. While, without question, there is much that can and must be learned from lecturers, classrooms, and note taking, there is just some knowledge of the most basic nature that can be gained only from personal experience; we learn by doing. Is there possibly a correlation between the fizzling in life of some high school and college graduates and knowledge heard versus truth internalized?

Quite often I tell young people that there is no particular power or charm tied up in a diploma. Of course its possession may give you a little more prestige to begin with. But life, real life, the kind of thing for which you think you are preparing, whether in or out of college, discloses its secret opportunities and joys only to those who have developed power through the facing of obstacles.

So I say, go to school, go to college if you can possibly get there. But while there, remember that there is no substitute for hard knocks. Whether in or out of college, we must enroll in the university whose colors are black and blue and whose song is something like, "Work, for the night is coming."

I close with a brief list of some course titles offered at old HKU.

Undergraduate Level

1. No success formula will work unless you do. (2 credits)
2. The daily grind of hard work gives a man polish. (2 credits)
3. Hard work is the yeast that raises the dough. (2 credits)

Graduate Level

4. The biggest room in the world is the room for improvement. (3 credits)
5. The person who is not fired with enthusiasm might get fired otherwise. (3 credits)

Chapter 22

Mistakes

I am thinking of two incidents, neither of which is very important, but together, at least to me, they are significant.

An acquaintance and I went into a restaurant together. As the waitress was serving our soup, her hand caught on the back of a chair, one of the dishes skidded a couple of inches, and several drops of the soup fell on my friend's coat sleeve.

"Stupid waitress!" he said, not aloud to her but in a sneering tone that he hoped she would hear. "Where do they find such stupid workers?"

The waitress was very sorry, as anyone could see by observing her anxious expression, and she immediately did everything that she could to relieve the situation. But my friend, who himself had occasionally made mistakes in his own work, made no effort to re-

trieve his unkind words and only left a cold dime tip
by his plate. (I added a couple of dollars when he was
not looking.) The waitress now had a cloud that
would put a shadow on her heart for the rest of the
day.

On another occasion, a highly respected business
executive, well known in the community, was standing before a counter in a drugstore. He was not re-
ceiving the attention that he felt he deserved. When
the clerk finally came to wait on him, he showed his
impatience and displeasure by uttering several unkind, harsh words. Many nice things that he could
have said with a little added humor and a smile—this
man who had worked his way up from a lowly position himself—were left unsaid as he grabbed his
package and stormed out of the store, leaving a
human soul with a feeling of discontent.

Jo Ann Larsen, a practicing family therapist says,
"Every day every one of the 5 billion people on this
planet makes a mistake. No one is exempt. It is the
nature of the human condition for people to flub—
regularly—as they stretch and grow in this life."

Let's face it, we have all been guilty of human
error at one time or another. I know I have. In my
moments of weakness I have often remembered the
thought, "Of all sad words of tongue or pen the saddest are these, it might have been." A hundred times
I have said to myself, "Oh, if I had just done it
another way. If I had just said the other word, but
now it is impossible to bring it back." We can certainly apologize. We can certainly realize that it
would be so much better if we could control ourselves
before the mistake occurs in the first place, but I
guess one of the real questions is how do we get rid of
the terrible feelings about these things that have happened in the past so that we can move forward with

grace and confidence. You are perhaps familiar with the words of one great man who said, as he looked back at many of his past mistakes, "Forgetting the things that are behind, I press forward."

That is more easily said than done, but Dr. Larsen relates examples of how two mothers were able to help their children handle these very challenges. She tells of one of the mothers who allowed each of her several children to make ten mistakes a day. In her own words the mother said: "One day my kids were carrying in the groceries and one of them dropped a bag. A big bottle of spaghetti sauce broke and splattered all over. My child pointed out the obvious: 'Mom, I made a BIG mess!' To which I responded, 'That's OK, we all get to make ten mistakes a day.' 'But I've already made five,' he observed. 'Well, this just makes six,' I said. That put a big smile on his face."

The second mother stated, "I've tried to deal with my children's mistakes with humor. Just recently, my son (who has four younger sisters and doesn't get along with them that well) came bombarding down the stairs, shouting, 'I'm so sick of these sisters! They're always getting into my stuff. I want a padlock on the door!'

"However, just before he [had shown] up, I had gone into the laundry room and I saw that he had taken all the clean laundry and thrown it on the floor, looking for a shirt. I was mad about it, but I didn't say anything while he was talking. I just counted to ten.

"[After he had thrown the clothes on the floor], he went back upstairs, came back down and said the same thing to me about his sisters. I looked at him and very calmly said, 'I know just how you feel. Someone went into the laundry room and pulled all the clean clothes out of the dryer! It makes me so mad, I guess I'll just have to put a padlock on the laundry room door!' That brought him to a screeching halt, and we were both able to laugh about the situation." (From the manuscript of Jo Ann Larsen's forthcoming book *I'm a Day Late and a Dollar Short, and It's OK: A Woman's Survival Guide for the '90s,* due for publication in 1991 by Deseret Book Co.)

I think those are practical approaches.

Since the mistakes we make cannot usually be recalled once they are committed anyway, then perhaps one of the ways to forget, after feeling regret and doing all we can about it, is to turn the uncomfortable feeling into more positive outlooks and sometimes use a little humor.

Most of us learn more from our own mistakes than we do from good examples set by others. The trail of advancement for everyone is strewn with unpleasant mistakes, because about the only way to achieve anything new and greater is through the trial-and-error method. Often the greatest mistake we can make is to continually fear that we will make one, but the individual who never makes mistakes seldom makes any progress. And remember, a fault recognized is already half-corrected.

I was reading the other day about the life of one of the movie screen's greatest actors. After every performance he would sit down by himself and ask the question, Why did I hold my audience so well? or, Why did I not hold them as well tonight as usual? And without worrying much about what had happened, he considered every mistake that he had made as an opportunity to learn something new for the next time. In like manner a close friend of mine, a professional athlete, carefully studies film clips of each of his performances for hours after every contest to see how he could improve.

Successful people are not afraid to make mistakes. They accept their errors and failures and continue on, knowing that making a mistake is a natural consequence of trying. Nelson Boswell says, ''The difference between greatness and mediocrity is often how an individual views a mistake.'' Remember, making a mistake is not as important as how you react to it. Elbert Hubbard adds, ''God will not look you over for medals, degrees, or diplomas, but for scars.''

Something that has always brought comfort to me as I have agonized over and tried to forget a past unfortunate event is knowing that many of the greatest people in the world have erred and continue to err, but they keep pursuing and achieving their goals anyway. You will recall that Columbus started his journey with very erroneous ideas, but he discovered America. (In that regard, I often have said to my family that when Columbus started his journey he didn't know where he was going; when he got there, he didn't know where he was; and when he returned he didn't know where he had been.) Sir Isaac Newton wrote a book, *Observations Upon the Prophecies of Daniel and the Apocalypse of St. John*, which he considered to be a marvelous treatise, yet it is known today as a theological crossword puzzle. But in spite of this, a scientific epoch is named after Newton. John Wesley, the theologian, founder of the Methodist church, was convinced that if he had to give up belief in witchcraft he would have to give up the Bible. (What a silly, mistaken idea!) And yet it was John Wesley who breathed the breath of a new life into a socially sick England. Joan of Arc, Martin Luther, and a host of similar individuals have given birth to new concepts and eras that would be laughed out of court by unlettered men of our time. But regardless of all their foolish, mistaken ideas, these personalities stand today among the great leaders of all time in the onward march of civilization.

Now, let's face up to it. Isn't it a fact that you and I often feel like giving up the whole thing? And we sometimes tell ourselves that we probably won't amount to anything because we have made so many blunders. Well, remember, the fellow who makes good isn't the one who never makes a mistake.

I picked up this little jingle which isn't very good poetry but which contains a very helpful thought:

> The man who never makes mistakes
>   And never guesses wrong,
> Who never any chances takes,
>   Works cautiously along,
> May never lose a single bone,
>   A dollar have to pay—
> Because he'll never likely own
>   A dollar anyway.
>
> The man who was never known to err
>   Will hold his job for years.
> He need not start, he need not stir,
>   Discharge he never fears.
> He sticks to old accustomed paths
>   As he has always done;
> He'll never lose the job he has,
>   Nor get a better one.

Chapter 23

Convenient
Christianity

We live in an age designed for convenient existence. We don't like to be bothered with anything that's not convenient. We like prepackaged dinners that can be done in a microwave oven in three minutes. We like remote control units that allow us to change the TV station without getting up from our seats. We like popcorn that pops and is buttered all in one unit, and we like permanent press that makes ironing boards a thing of the past. Convenience. That's the criterion we use for making so many choices in life. Is it convenient?

Well, that may be fine and good where many choices are concerned. Life is complex enough that anything that makes it more convenient is surely a blessing. But it is also so simple to let the standard of convenience govern our every choice, that we are asking ourselves, "Is it easy?" about very important things. Can I do it without strain? Will it bother me? Or in other words—Is it convenient?

We may even start to ask these kinds of questions about our values and morals. In a me-oriented society, it is easy to consider religion mainly in terms of how easily we can work its precepts into our schedules. What a dangerous mind-set that can be, because Christianity—that set of eternal laws that we know corresponds to the way things really are—isn't always convenient. It's not easy to forsake the mindless pleasure of the moment to develop a more noble character. It's not convenient to stand up for unchanging values in an immoral world. And, most painful of all, it's never easy to give your time or your means to another when it seems you hardly have enough of either for yourself.

Of all the hard doctrines Christianity sets up for the believer, is there any more challenging than plain, old-fashioned charity? It seems so often that it just doesn't work into your schedule, right? Sometimes it means sacrifice and bother and displacing number one from the center of your thoughts—which is never easy. Sometimes there is, in giving, a certain amount of giving up.

Take the experience of the high school student who was struggling somewhat with his grades. An active boy, he participated in a number of sports, belonged to a musical group, had a paper route, and had two other part-time jobs.

One day when he was feeling under the weather, his mother took him to see the family doctor. Following a physical exam, the doctor said to him, "You're involved in too many activities and you are going to have to give something up."

"Very well," said the young man, "I'll see about dropping out of school at once!" That's some sacrifice!

But sometimes we are the same way about the things we are willing to do for others. For someone else we'd do anything, as long as it doesn't mean giving of our time, our money, our effort, or our thought. We'd give anything else—but certainly not those.

Elijah, the prophet, as you may remember, entered a city and there by the city gate saw a widow who was gathering sticks. He called to her and said, "Fetch me, I pray thee, a little water in a vessel, that I may drink." And as she was going to get it, the prophet enlarged his request. "Bring me, I pray thee, a morsel of bread," he added.

She answered in these pathetic words, "As the Lord thy God liveth, I have not a cake, but an handful of meal in a barrel, and a little oil in a cruse: and, behold, I am gathering two sticks, that I may go in and dress it for me and my son, that we may eat it, and die." Now, it would be more than inconvenient for her to give something to another. One would think the word *impossible* would be a more likely description.

But Elijah persisted in his wanting food from her. He said he still wanted her to make him a cake. What must she have thought in that moment? "What nerve! Is this man crazy? Has he no ears to hear?" But Elijah went on with a wonderful promise for her if she would serve him though it seemed manifestly inconvenient to do so. He said that her barrel of meal should not run out nor her cruse of oil fail until the Lord sent rain to restore them, and the Bible concludes the story with this understated little summary of what must have been a glorious miracle, "And she, and he, and her house, did eat many days." (1 Kings 17:10–16.)

If one is willing to give what he has to another, the Lord more than amply repays. And the truth is, we must be willing and ready to give to others, because when they need help that's when they need it, not some other time. We can't wait to work them into our schedule the fourth Friday of the second month of next year when we happen to have a break. We can't wait until everything seems completed and orderly in our own lives before we stretch ourselves into the life of another. Things don't ever really settle down. Charity never really becomes convenient. There is always something else and then something else again to do.

A family I know that lives on the coast had been very concerned about the starving people of southeastern Asia. They had looked with anguished hearts at the pictures in news magazines of mothers holding emaciated children. They had read every detail they could find about the refugee camps and the various attempts to get food into the people. They were heartsick that others were suffering.

But you know, it is easy to feel those undirected charitable feelings, and having felt them, believe yourself cleansed of the duty to do anything. Such was this young couple. They said to themselves, "If we could ever do anything for any of those people, we surely would. You bet, we would." It was vaguely comforting to them, and I suspect they felt quite righteous for their loving sentiments.

But then their charity and their Christianity were put to a real test. One of the refugee foundations called them unexpectedly and said that a planeload of Laotian refugees had arrived in their city from southeastern Asia that very day, and they did not have an adequate number of sponsors lined up for the families. A family of three was waiting there in the office with no place to go, no place to sleep that very night. Would the young couple sponsor them?

Of course the husband wanted to know what being a sponsor entailed. The answer was overwhelming. They were to put the family up and feed them. They were to find them jobs and an apartment. They were to help them furnish their apartment and get food. They were to see that they got health checkups and got into school. The adults were to be signed up for English classes. The list went on and on.

So the husband called his wife, and they talked. How in the world could they possibly sponsor a family? They had four children under the age of six. The husband was just starting his own business and was gone almost every evening. They were so busy. After all their worried feelings about the problems in southeastern Asia, when it came right down to involving them personally, well, it was inconvenient. It just wouldn't work out. But they did agree to one thing. They couldn't let the family spend their first night in America sleeping on an office floor. They would let them stay in their home for just two or three days until another sponsor family could be found.

But you know, the kind of love we call Christian charity is not only inconvenient, it's joyful. It makes all those other urgencies look so trivial in comparison. After three days, this couple couldn't bear to stop helping their Laotian family. It would have been painful to pass them on to another sponsor family, sending them rootless again into the world. The couple couldn't say a word to their Laotian family that they could understand, but between them there was a communication that was far deeper than language. It wasn't always easy. How do you tell someone to come for breakfast when they don't understand what breakfast means? How do you serve spaghetti to Laotians, knowing all the time that it falls far short of their favorite food?

Yes, it was inconvenient—hard to find a job for a non-English speaker, hard to find the time to hunt for an apartment. But the whole inconvenient, joyful experience was summed up in one incident. The American family had told their Laotian family over and over again that they loved them, even though they knew they didn't understand a word. And one bright day, the Laotian daughter turned back to the young couple and said her first sentence in perfect English. "I love *you*," she said.

And that's the way it is with Christian charity, the kind of love that penetrates all barriers. It starts out looking inconvenient and winds up leading you to the most important moments of your life. In a world of convenience living, may you and I dare to do the inconvenient, to serve someone else—even if it doesn't fit into our schedules.

...and then some

Chapter 24

. . . *And Then Some*

W_{alk} with light." It's one of the most beautiful lines in the English language. I don't know who wrote it, but as used here, it suggests the blessing of being filled with a knowledge and understanding of truth, of wisdom, of enlightenment. Interestingly, we can read the exact same phrase posted on traffic signals at city street intersections all over the country, and in this sense, it clearly gives instruction for our safety. Though the two usages of this meaningful thought seem to serve different purposes, I think they basically are saying the same thing—we need and surely desire to be edified and enriched in all areas of our lives for the greatest and most satisfactory achievement possible in our various endeavors.

Over the years I have learned that wisdom comes more often from living than from studying, and in the preceding pages I have shared, in the form of my own and others' personal experiences, some of the truth, wisdom, and enlightenment I have been privileged to gain.

A wise man has said:

> Do more than exist, live.
> Do more than touch, feel.
> Do more than look, observe.
> Do more than read, absorb.
> Do more than hear, listen.
> Do more than think, ponder.
>
> John Rhodes

The secret, then, of real success can be summed up in just three words: . . . *And then some.* I have discovered that most of the difference between average people and top people can be explained, again, in those same three words.

The top people do what is expected of them—and then some. They are thoughtful and considerate of others—and then some. They meet their obligations and responsibilities fairly and squarely—and then some. They are good friends to their friends—and then some. They can be counted on in an emergency —and then some.

So it is when you serve people and the Lord, when you are striving to know, to be, and to do all that you can: the Lord pays in full—and then some.

Index